H.P. Smith

A Collection of Coins and Medals

H.P. Smith

A Collection of Coins and Medals

ISBN/EAN: 9783742818256

Manufactured in Europe, USA, Canada, Australia, Japa

Cover: Foto ©Lupo / pixelio.de

Manufactured and distributed by brebook publishing software
(www.brebook.com)

H.P. Smith

A Collection of Coins and Medals

A COLLECTION

OF

COINS & MEDALS,

INCLUDING SOME SCARCE

AMERICAN & ANCIENT GOLD,

TOGETHER WITH

GREEK AND ROMAN SILVER AND BRONZE:

Rare Patterns

OF THE UNITED STATES,

Books, Papers, etc.

TO BE SOLD AT AUCTION,

BY

BANGS & CO.,

739 and 741 Broadway, New York City,

At 2 o'Clock, P. M.,

Thursday and Friday, July 27=28, 1882.

Bids will be executed by the Auctioneers, and by all reputable Coin Dealers throughout the country.

CATALOGUED BY

H. P. SMITH, 269 W. 52d St., N. Y. City.

CATALOGUE.

—•—

FOREIGN COPPER COINS, ETC.

1 Irish and Scotch Farthings of Charles I. One pierced, one edge broken. Fair lot   4 pieces

2 Gun Money. James II. Shillings, March and June. Edges not quite perfect, one edge reeded. Good to fine   2 pcs

3 Same. XXX Pence. Corroded. Fair

4 1791. East India Co. ½, ¼, ⅛ Anna. V. E. I. C. within heart-shaped shield. ⅛ above, date below. Rev., Balance, Hindoo-stanee characters. *Beautiful bronze proofs.*   4 pieces

5 Same. ½ cent, ½ Anna (2) varieties. Good   3 pieces

6 1793. Georgivs III. Bust. Rev., "Bermuda" ship and date. Penny. Cleaned. Very fine

7 1797. Penny. George III. Letters countersunk. Cleaned. Very good

8 1806. Georgins III. halfpenny. Rev., Bahama. Ship, etc. Cleaned. Very fine

9 1821. St. Helena halfpenny. Cleaned. Very fine

10 1813, '39. Geo. III., Victoria. Farthing, halfpenny and penny. Isle of Man. Penny, letters countersunk. Good to fine   3 pieces

11 Melbourne. Annand Smith & Co. penny token. Obv., Britannia seated. Fine

12 Victoria, William IIII. half-farthings (2) ⅓ farthings (4). Cleaned. Good lot   6 pieces

13 Model ¼ farthings, 1848. Cleaned. Very small   2 pieces

14 Model penny. White centre, Victoria. Good

15 1879. Cyprus, ½, ¼ piastre. Uncirculated. Partially bright. Desirable   2 pieces

16 1669. Chester farthing. England. Good for period

17 1870. Ceylon, ¼, ½, 1 and 5 cents. The 1 partially bright; the 5 bright, the others good. Desirable   4 pieces

18 1830, '34. Guernesey 1, 4, 8 doubles. Good lot   3 pieces

19 1859, '60. Pennies of Victoria. Large and small. Canada cents (2). 3 bright. Uncirculated   4 pieces

20 1852. J. Barnard, Norwich. Rooster and hen. Rev., Farm scene, dealer in game, etc. Bright. Uncirculated

21 Trinidad, St. Domingo, Antigua. Farthings. Good lot   3 pieces

22 Venice and two coins struck by Knights of Malta. Fair lot   3 pieces

23 1794. Daniel Eccleston, Lancaster. Halfpenny. Raised rim, letters countersunk. Proof

24 Pidcock's Exhibition. Obv., Elephant. Farthing. Good

25 Liverpool Exchange Club 3ᵈ, Pack Horse Inn, Corsham; 2ᵈ Truro, 1830. Obv., Lion, "Paid." Good and fine   3 pieces

26 Turkey. Two copper coins. Size 24. Nearly good   2 pcs

27 Tunis and Turkey. Small and large. 1 pierced. Tunis base silver. Fair to fine   7 pieces

28 Japan. 1 Rin. 1, 2, Sen. Uncirculated. Bright and partially bright   3 pieces

29 Hong Kong, 1 Mil; Japan, 1 Rin (3). Bright. Uncirculated   4 pieces

30 1847. Republic Liberia. Palm tree. One cent. Fine

31 1847. Hapa Haneri; only coin Sandwich Islands. Cleaned. Fine

32 1863. Sarawak, one cent, J. Brooke, Rajah. Dark. Good

33 Peru. ¼ de peso; Mexico Cuartilla de real. Good and barely fair   2 pieces

34 1745, '87, '90, '93. Stad Utricht, Zelandia, etc. Fair to fine   5 pieces

35 Mantua. Siege piece. Un soldo. Very good. Desirable

36 Sweden. Chas. XII. Daler's. Good lot   8 pieces

37 Peru, Venezuela 1 and dos centavo. Very fine   2 pieces

38 Honduras, provisional 4 real. Barely fair   3 pieces

39 French Turnois, 1608, etc. Fair to good   7 pieces

40 1722 to 1866. Mostly old dates. Papal coin. Baiocco, Mezzo Baiocco, ½ soldo, etc. Desirable lot. Fair to very fine   14 pieces

41 Sicily. Ferdinand II. Tornesi Dieci. Very fair

42 1851, '54. Russia ¼, ½, 1 2) kopeck. Fine   4 pieces

43 1796. Sierra Leone Company. Lion. Rev., Hands clasped. One cent piece. Cleaned. Nearly good

44 Ships, Colonies and Commerce. English flag. Bright. Uncirculated   5 pieces

45 Maximilian Centavo. Mexico. Fair

46 Quebec. Mason Jacques Cartier, St. Roch. Beaver. Rev., Un Centin Payable, etc. Uncir. Bright. Desirable

47 Siberia 2 Kopeck, Morocco Centime, One Quart Giteralter, William and William et Mary Farthings. Fair to Uncirculated   6 pieces

48 Cartagena, Guiana, Mexico, Sumatra and other queer and interesting coin   25 pieces

49 English, etc., Farthings, Halfpenny and Penny Tokens. Some desirable pieces. Average very good   27 pieces

50 Miscellaneous lot coins, all different. None pierced. Fair to very fine   160 pieces

51 Same. All different. None pierced   50 pieces

52 Another lot. Contains duplicates. Poor to fine   243 pieces

53 1863. Copper Head Tokens. Unassorted lot. Contains numerous pieces that are bright and uncirculated. 190 pcs

U. S. SILVER DOLLARS.

The No. has reference to Haseltine's Type Table Catalogue, without guarantee. It will be seen that they are not given in his order. The collection contains some very fine pieces, and where catalogued as fine or very fine, the stars are mostly sharp.

54 1795. Flowing hair. No. 12. Slight defect in edge of planchet. Strongly struck. Barely circulated. Polished surface. Desirable

55 1795. Same. No. 1. Nicked. Trifle weak at one place on the rev. Very good

56 1795. Same. No. 2. Two or three trifling file marks on bust. The stars fronting face large ; behind head they are much smaller. Three different sized stars on this obv. Fine

57 1795. Same. No. 7. Small nick on edge. Very fine

7.0 58 1795. Same. No. 5. Better than fine

/ 3.0 59 1795. Same. No. 1. Very good

' 2.5⁻ 60 1795. Same. No. 6. Fine

/ 3.0 61 1795. Same. No. 5. Obv. file marks. Fine. Rev. very
good indeed

2 .0 62 1795. Fillet head. No. 14. Fine

/ 4.0 63 1795. Duplicate. Nicked. Good

/ 2.5⁻ 64 1795. Same. Very fair indeed

/ 3.5⁻ 65 1795. Same. No. 15. Piece nicked from edge. Nearly
fine

2 1.0 66 1796. Large date. No. 5. Minute scratches on bust.
Nearly fine. Desirable

2 0.5⁻ 67 1796. Small date. No. 1. Rev. weaker than obv. Nearly
fine

2 1.0⁻ 68 1796. Same. No. 4. Barely circulated. Lustre

/ 5.5⁻ 69 1796. Duplicate. Nicked. Very good indeed

2 5.0 70 1797. Six stars facing. No. 3. Strongly struck. Nicked.
Very fine. Desirable

2 1.5⁻ 71 1797. Duplicate. Very good

2 .50 72 1797. Same. Trifle scratched and blurred. Very good

/ 4.0 73 1798. Large eagle. No. 21. Branch has 5 berries, not
mentioned by H. Extremely fine. Lustre

, 4.0 74 1798. Same. No. 17. Very fine. Lustre

/ 2.5⁻ 75 1798. Same. (Can't find combination.) Ten arrows; two
sticks. One place on rev. trifle weak. Very fine indeed

2.5⁻ 76 1798. Same. No. 13. Nicked. Fine

/ 2.5⁻ 77 1798. Same. No. 28. Very fine indeed

/ 2.0 78 1798. Same. No. 18. Very fine indeed

/ 1.0 79 1798. Same. No. 28. Beginning made to pierce on rev.
Very good

/ 2.4 80 1798. Same. No. 21. Nicked. Nearly fine

/ 1.5⁻ 81 1798. Same. No. 10. Rough planchet, by stars back of
head and by Lib. Very fine

, 5.0 82 1798. Same. No. 13. Extremely fine. Lustre

/ 2.5⁻ 83 1798. Same. Break in die from E of Liberty to 7 of date.
Not mentioned by H. Very good

/ 1.5⁻ 84 1798. Same. No. 11. Nicked. Fine

2.5⁻ 85 1798. Same. No. 29. Break in die does not extend to 9.
File marks or scratches on Rev. Very fine

' 86 1798. Same. No. 28. Some stars on rev. weak. Good

87 1798. Same. Obv., No. 17 ; Rev., No. 10. Fine. Desirable if the combination is correct

88 1798. Same. No. 26. Edge trifle abused. Good

89 1798. Same. No. 6. Rev. scratched ; Obv. fine

90 1798. Same. No. 3. Good

91 1798. Same. No. 18. Very fine. Lustre

92 1798. Same. No. 24. About good

93 1799. 5 stars facing. No 23. Abused. Very fair

94 1799 over 98. No. 3. Rev., 15 stars, two just emerging from under clouds. Fine

95 1799. Duplicate of last. Somewhat better

96 1799. Same. No. 2. Rev., No. 3. Star cut before mouth. 15 stars and cracked die on Rev. Nearly fine

97 1799. Think this a duplicate of last. Fine

98 1799. This is over 98. Has 15 stars on the Rev., and is a beautiful piece. Desirable

99 1799. No. 16. Barely circulated. Desirable

100 1799. No. 9. Well struck. Rev. shows scratches. Stars very sharp. Very fine

101 1799. No. 10. Well struck. Extremely fine. Lustre

102 1799. No. 6. Strongly struck. Extremely fine. Lustre

103 1799. No. 4. Obv. shows badly cracked die ; Rev., 15 stars, 2 of them nearly invisible under the clouds. Edge, minute nick. Very fine

104 1799. No. 9. Very good

105 1799. No. 11. Very fine

106 1799. No. 16. Trifle nicked. Very fine indeed

107 1799. No. 4. With slight differences. Barely circulated

108 1799. No. 17. Very fine indeed

109 1799. No. 16. Very good

110 1799. No. 6. Very fine

111 1799. No. 16. Obv. die much broken. Very fine

112 1799. No. 4. Trifling defect on edge. Very fine

113 1799. No. 17. Minute scatches. Very fine

114 1799. No. 9. Very fine

115 1799. No. 8. About fine

116 1799. No. 9. Slight scratches on Rev. Fine

117 1799. No. 17. Nicked. Very fine

118 1799. No. 6. Very fair

119 1799. No. 17. Very fine

2 5 120 1799. No. 22. Very fine

/ 2 5 121 1799. No. 17. Very fine

/ 3 ᴗ 122 1800. No. 14. Break in die through first 0 of date. Very fine

ᴗ ᴗ 123 1800. No. 16. This is said to be the comet variety, from the fact that there is a break in the die from eagle's wing through O F. Like tail of comet. Very fine. Desirable

/ 4 ᴗ 124 1800. No. 11. Very fine

/ 4 ᴗ 125 1800. No. 1. Very fine

/ ᴗ 0 126 1800. No. 4. Very fine

/ 3 ᴗ 127 1800. No. 8. Very fine

3 5 128 1800. No. 16. Comet more distinct. Very good indeed

/ ᴗ ᴗ 129 1800. No. 1. Very fine

/ 4 ᴗ 130 1800. No. 11. Fine

/ 3 ᴗ 131 1801. No. 1. Edge trifle abused ; trifle nicked. Good

, 8 5 132 1801. No. 2. Nick by last 1 of date. Fine

/ 3 ᴗ 133 1802 over 1. No. 2. Nicks. Very fine

/ 4 5 134 1802 over 1. No. 4. Nicked. Fine

/ 5 ᴗ 135 1802. No. 6. Fine

/ 5 ᴗ 136 1802. No. 6. Very good

/ 5 5 137 1803. Crooked 3. No. 4. Good

' 6 5 138 1803. Variety of crooked 3. No. 5. Fine

2 ᴗᴗ 139 1803. Large 3. No. 6. Very fine

2 5 ᴗ 140 1838. Beautiful electrotype of this scarce and desirable dollar

/ / ᴗ 141 1843. Circulated proof. Very fine

/ ᴗ 5 142 1844. Nicked. Some polish. Very fine

/ / 2 143 1845. Circulated proof. Very fine

/ / 5 144 1846. Extremely fine. Mint lustre

2 5 145 1847. Uncirculated. Proof surface. Desirable

/ 2 ᴗ 146 1850. Polished surface. Pin scratches. Very fine

/ 3 ᴗ 147 1853. Nicked. Very fine

/ 3 ᴗ 148 1853. Nicked. Very good

5 8 5 149 1854. Nicked. Very good indeed

3 2 5 5 150 1855. BRILLIANT PROOF. In this condition a dollar of this date is more desirable than a dollar of 1858, for the reason that ten of 1858 turn up, while one of this date is rarely heard of. A proof set of this date without the Quarter sold for $61.00 in the Bushnell sale ; if this dollar sells in the same proportion it ought to bring $50.00

⊃⌐⌐ 151 1855. Very fine indeed and desirable
⊂ ⌐⌐ 152 1856. Barely circulated. Trifling nicks. Lustre
⊂ ⌐⌐ 153 1857. Proof. Minute nicks in field; in this condition a
    very desirable coin
⌐⌐ 154 1859. N. O. Very fine indeed. Strongly struck
⌐⌐ 155 1860. Fine proof. Desirable
⌐⌐ 156 1863. Brilliant proof
⌐⌐ 157 1865. Nicked. Very good
⌐⌐ 158 1868. Trifling nicks. Fine polished surface
⌐⌐ 159 1870. Trifling blemished proof
⌐⌐ 160 1873. Trade. Very fine indeed. Lustre
⌐⌐ 161 1874. Uncirculated. Brilliant
⌐⌐ 162 1875. Brilliant proof. Chafed a little in field
⌐⌐ 163 1879. Bland. Brilliant proof
⌐⌐ 164 1879. Trade. Brilliant proof
⌐⌐ 165 1880. Bland. Brilliant proof
⌐⌐ 166 1880. N. O. Small o. Bland. Uncirculated. Lustre
⌐⌐ 167 1880. Trade. Brilliant proof
⌐⌐ 168 1880. Same. Brilliant proof
⌐⌐ 169 1880. Duplicate

UNITED STATES CENTS AND HALF CENTS.

⌐⌐ 170 1793. Wreath. Electrotype. Very fine
⌐⌐ 171 1794. Maris, No. 2. In places weak. Nearly good
⌐⌐ 172 1794. Maris, No 9. Obv. fair; rev. barely fair
⌐⌐ 173 1794. Maris, No. 16. Strongly struck. Dark. Obv.
    planchet, trifle rough. Very fine indeed
⌐⌐ 174 1794. Maris, No. 17. Well struck. About fine
⌐⌐ 175 1794. Maris, No. 22. Minute scratches on face. Dark.
    Well struck. Very fine indeed
⌐⌐ 176 1794. Maris, No. 24. Dark. Barely circulated. Desirable
⌐⌐ 177 1794. Varieties. Poor to nearly good   3 pieces
  178 1797-98. Very fair and about good   2 pieces
  179 1802. Fair to nearly good   5 pieces
⌐⌐ 180 1805, '7 (2), '8 (2). Fair   5 pieces
⌐⌐ 181 1809. Stars all sharp but one or two. Date very strongly
    struck. Hair shows but little traces of wear. Dark.
    Very fine indeed. Desirable
⌐⌐ 182 1809. Rather poor   2 pieces

2 6 183 1810. Very fair and good   2 pieces
1 5-0 184 1811. Obv., planchet rough. Very fair
4 185 1812 (2); '15, altered, (2); one '15 a decided curiosity.
          Poor to very good   4 pieces
10 186 1815. Altered from '45. Well done. 16. Dark   2 pieces
40 187 1817. Uncirculated. Bright. Trifle smeared
5- 188 1818. Same. Spot over 18 of date
17 189 1819. Uncirculated. Bright. Obv. smeared; rev., spots
05- 190 1820. Small date. Perfect die. Cleaned. Perhaps uncir.
o 191 1821, '22 (3). Fair and very fair   4 pieces
6 192 1823 over 22. Very fair
10-0 193 1824. Stars nearly all sharp. Dark. Very fine indeed. A
          desirable cent in this condition
5- 194 1825, '26, '27 (2). Very fair to very good   4 pieces
7-0 195 1827. Cleaned and blackened, but little or no traces of cir-
          culation
3 196 1828. Large and small dates. 1 varnished. Fair to
          very fine   2 pieces
5- 197 1829. Dark. Stars sharp. Trifling blemish on edge. Fine
114 198 1829, (3), 30 (2), 31, 32 (2), 33. About good   9 pieces
5- 199 1834. Large date. Cracked die. Olive. Barely circulated
1 200 1834. Small. 35, 36. Very fair to good   3 pieces
12 201 1837. Plain hair strings. Olive. Smear. Extremely fine
30 202 1838. A few stars flat. Handsome color. Extremely fine.
          Desirable
5- 203 1838. Stars flat. Olive. Extremely fine
30 204 1839. The 4 varieties. Fair to fine   4 pieces
10 205 1840. Large and small. Dark. About fine   2 pieces
1 206 1841 (2), 43 (2), 44 (2), 45 (2). Very fair to fine. 2
          cleaned   8 pieces
1 207 1846. 47 (3), 48, 49. Good to fine. 1 cleaned   6 pieces
12 208 1847. Well struck. Very fine
5- 209 1850. Uncirculated. Redish bright
1 210 1850. 51 (2). Extremely fine   3 pieces
2 211 1852. Broad rim. Uncirculated. Partially bright
3 212 1852. Extremely fine and uncirculated   3 pieces
3 213 1853. Uncirculated and very fine   2 pieces
C 214 1854. Uncirculated. Some brightness
• 215 1853–54. Extremely fine   2 pieces
15 216 1855. Upright 5. Uncirculated. Brilliant

2 217 1855. Same. Bright. Uncirculated. Little smear
2 218 1855. Both varieties. Uncirculated. Partially bright. 2 pcs
6 219 1856. Both varieties. Very fine. Uncirculated. Bright 2 pcs
5 220 1857. Large date. About good
2 50 221 1856. NICKEL PATTERN. Brilliant proof
55 222 1793. HALF CENT. Planchet rough or corroded. Very
 good
5 223 1794. Rev. trifle misstruck. Very fine
5 224 1795. Thin. Black. Scratch on rev. Nearly good
37 225 1797. Has been abused, although but little circulated.
 Half cent on rev. does not show, nor Rty. Date plain
 and strong
65 226 1802. Black and oxydized. Very fair
2 227 1809 10. Good and fine   2 pieces
5 228 1811. Rev., little of wreath and a few letters flattened by a
 blow. Dark. Very fine. Desirable
55 229 1811. Nearly good
30 230 1811. Obv., scratched in field, both sides of bust. About
 good
3 231 1837. Half cent worth, etc. Extremely fine
5 231a Half cents. Various dates, 1 or 2 abused. Very fair to
 fine   24 pieces

UNITED STATES HALF DOLLARS.

Catalogued according to Hazeltine's Type Table. Same remarks as were
used in regard to the Dollars.

52 232 1794. No. 1. Nicked. Very fair
2 5 233 1794. Same. Five bad scratches on obv., otherwise very
 good impression
5 234 1795. No. 24. Nicked. Most all lines of hair showing.
 Very good
5 235 1795. No. 3. Better impression than the last
5 236 1795. No. 10. Beginning made to pierce on rev. Scratched.
 Good
5 237 1795. No. 8. A good impression
 238 1795. No. 20. Trifle scratched. Nearly fine
 239 1795. No. 5. Better condition than the last
 240 1795. No. 9. Nicked. Good

241 1795. Same. File marks on bust. Very fair indeed
242 1795. No. 10. Edge trifle imperfect. Very fair
243 1795. No. 7. Scratched on obv. Very fair
244 1795. No. 28. Cracked die on rev. Scratches. About good
245 1795. No. 8. Scratched a little. Good
246 1801. No. 1. Small V cut on bust. Nearly good
247 1801. Same. A fair impression
248 1802. No. 1. Nicked. Nearly good
249 1802. Same. Trifle better than the last
250 1803. No. 3. Very fine indeed. Desirable
251 1803. Same. Not equal to the last. Fine
252 1803. No. 2. Very good
253 1803. Same. Nicked. Same condition
254 1803. No. 1. Obv. better. Rev. not as good as last
255 1803. No. 3. Very good
256 1803. No. 2. Nicked. Trifle better than last
257 1803. Same. Condition the same
258 1803. Same. Same
259 1803. Same. Condition about the same
260 1803. No. 3. Very good
261 1803. No. 4. Crooked 3. Nearly good
262 1803. Same. Nicked. Very good
263 1803. Duplicate. About good
264 1805 over 4. No. 1. Nearly good. Desirable
265 1805. No. 8. Nicked. Very good
266 1805. No. 9. Nicked. Better than the last
267 1805. No. 10. Very good
268 1805. No. 11. Nicked. Fine
269 1806. Blunt 6. No. 11. Nicked. Nearly good
270 1806. Same. No. 11. Abused. About fine
271 1806. Same. No. 11. Good
272 1807. Head to right. No. 2. Very fine indeed. Lustre. Desirable
273 1807. Same. No. 2. Beginning made to pierce on the rev. Very fine
274 1807. Same. No. 2. Very fine. Desirable
275 1807. Head to left. No. 9. Good
276 1807. Same. No. 9. Somewhat better
277 1808. No. 3. Very good
278 1809. No. 2. Barely circulated. Desirable

 279 1810. No. 3. Nicked. Fine
 280 1811. No. 1. Extremely fine. Lustre
 281 1812. No. 2. Sharp. Uncirculated. Minute nick on
      edge
 282 1812. No. 3. Very good indeed
 283 1813. No. 2. Very fine
 284 1814. No. 2. Very fine indeed
 285 1815. Very good
 286 1815. About good
 287 1815. Nearly the same
 288 1815. Little scratched. Very fair
 289 1817. No. 3. Barely circulated. Lustre
 290 1818 over 17. No. 2. Very fine indeed. Lustre
 291 1818. No. 12. Extremely fine. Lustre
 292 1818. No. 6. The open eight. Fine. Desirable
 293 1819. No. 10. Very fine indeed
 294 1819. No. 6. Extremely fine. Lustre
 295 1820 over 19. No. 1. Very good
 296 1820. Large date. No. 4. Very fine indeed. Polished sur-
      face.
 297 1821. No. 1. Extremely fine. Lustre
 298 1822. No. 7. Very fine indeed. Lustre
 299 1824. No. 4. Very fine indeed
 300 1824. No. 6. Extremely fine. Lustre
 301 1825. No. 11. Uncirculated. Lustre
 302 1825. No. 6. Extremely fine. Lustre
 303 1826. No. 4. Extremely fine. Lustre
 304 1826. No. 8. Very fine indeed. Lustre
 305 1827. No. 4. Very fine indeed. Lustre
 306 1827. No. 8. Uncirculated. Lustre
 307 1827. Curled 2. No. 11. Uncirculated. Lustre. Desirable
 308 1828. Large date. Curled 2. No. 4. Uncirculated. Lustre
      Desirable
 309 1828. Same. No. 1. Good
 310 1828. Same. No. 2. Good
 311 1828. Same. No. 6. Fair
 312 1828. Straight 2. Extremely fine. Lustre
 313 1829. Close date. Not described by H. Extremely fine.
      Lustre
 314 1829. No. 12. Uncirculated. Lustre

315 1829. Same. Extremely fine. Lustre

316 1830. Large 0. Extremely fine. Lustre

317 1830. Small 0. Cracked die. Uncirculated. Lustre

318 1831. No. 6. Uncirculated. Lustre

319 1831. No. 1. Extremely fine. Lustre

320 1831. Same. Extremely fine. Lustre

321 1832. No. 6. Uncirculated. Lustre

322 1832. Same. Extremely fine. Lustre

323 1834. Small date. No. 7. Very fine indeed. Lustre

324 1835. No. 1. Uncirculated. Lustre

325 1835. No. 2. Uncirculated. Lustre

326 1836. Broad Milling, No. 4. Uncirculated. Lustre

327 1836. Reeded edge. Head like 37. No. 1, Nicked. Good and desirable

328 1837. No. 1. Extremely fine. Lustre

329 1837. Planchet thinner and broader than last lot. Extremely fine. Lustre

330 1837. Same as first 37. Cracked die. Extremely fine. Lustre

331 1838. Extremely fine

332 1838. Extremely fine. Lustre

333 1838. Very fine

334 1839. No. 1. Very fine indeed

335 1839. O under bust. No. 2. Trifling nick on obv. and rev. Very fine indeed and desirable

336 1839. Liberty seated. No. 1. Nicked. Fine

337 1840. No. 2. Uncirculated. Lustre

338 1840. Same. Duplicate

339 1841. N. O. and Philadelphia. Very good and fine   2 pcs

340 1842. Large and small. Fine and very fine   2 pieces

341 1843. Extremely fine. Lustre

342 1844-5. N. O. Good and fine   2 pieces

343 1846. Dutch 6. Very fine indeed. Lustre

344 1846. Yankee 6. Very fine. Lustre

345 1847. About fine

346 1848. Has a very fine polished surface, probably struck for a proof. It is one of the best half dollars of this date that I ever saw. Desirable

347 1848. N. O. Extremely fine. Lustre. Desirable

348 1849. Uncirculated. Lustre. Desirable

349 1850. N. O. Extremely fine. Lustre. Desirable
350 1851. Strongly struck. Nicked. Very fine indeed. Desirable
351 1851. N. O. Same as last
352 1851. Same. About good
353 1851. Same. Nearly the same   2 pieces
354 1852. Nicked. Good
355 1853. N. O. Stars all but one double struck. Very good
356 1854. N. O. and Philadelphia. Uncirculated. Lustre 2 pcs
357 1855. N. O. Extremely fine. Lustre
358 1858. Uncirculated. Lustre
359 1859. San Francisco. Small S. Very good
360 1860. Uncirculated. Lustre
361 1861. Brilliant proof
362 1861. Extremely fine. Lustre
363 1861. N. O. Uncirculated. Lustre. Desirable
364 1863. Brilliant proof
365 1866. Brilliant proof. Trifle blemished
366 1866. San Francisco. Without "In God," etc. Very fair
         3 pieces
367 1867. Brilliant proof
368 1867. Very fine. Proof polish
369 1868. Brilliant proof
370 1872 Brilliant proof. Trifle blemished
371 1873. Arrow heads. Uncirculated. Lustre
372 1874. Brilliant proof
373 1874. San Francisco. Uncirculated. Lustre. Desirable
374 1875. Uncirculated. Lustre
375 1877. San Francisco. Extremely fine. Lustre
376 1879. Uncirculated. Lustre
377 1879. Duplicate
378 1879. Another. Same condition
379 1879. Same
380 1879. Duplicate

ANCIENT GREEK AND ROMAN SILVER COINS.

381 Corinth. Didrachm. Head of Pallas. Rev., Pegasus to left. Very good
382 Heraclea. Didrachm. Head of Pallas. Rev., Hercules with club, etc. Fair

383 Velia. Didrachm. Scylla on helmet of Pallas. Rev., A lion to left. Good

384 Dyrrachium. Drachm. ΑΝΤΙΓΟΝΟΣ above cow and calf. Rev., Gardens of Alcinous. Very fair

385 Macedonia. Drachm of Alexander Magnus; and Heimdrachm of Sicyon. Poor and fair   2 pieces

386 Consular Denarii. Antonia. Obv., War galley; M. Ant. Aug. Rev., Army standards; Legions IV., V. and VIII. Fair and good   3 pieces

387 Cornelia. Denarius of P. Sula; Victory in a biga. Also, one of Furia; head of Janus. Rev., Pallas crowning a trophy. Good   2 pieces

388 Pompeia. Rev., Wolf nursing the twins, discovered by Faustulus under the fig tree. Also, one of Papiria. Rev., Jupiter Fulminator in a quadriga. Very good. Denarii   2 pieces

389 68 A. D. Nero. Denarius. Head to right. Rev., Nero standing. Very good

390 117 A. D. Trajan and Hadrian. Rev., Mars and Justice. Good   2 pieces

391 180 A. D. Marcus Aurelius. Fine portrait. Rev., Victory holding a shield inscribed "Vic. Par." Sharp and desirable

392 211 A. D. Septimus Severus. Fine portraits, with titles Britannicus and Parthicus. Revs., Sev. at a tripod altar, and Jupiter between Caracalla and Geta. Fine   2 pieces

393 211 A. D. Septimus Severus. Revs., Annona and Mars. Good   2 pieces

394 217 A. D. Caracalla. An exceedingly fine portrait. Rev., Venus Victrix. Uncirculated and sharp

395 212 A. D. Fulvia Plantilla. Fine portrait. Rev., Cupid at feet of Venus. Very good

396 217 A. D. Julia Domna. Fine portraits. Rev., Juno and Diana Lucifera. Fine   2 pieces

397 212 A. D. Geta. Busts as infant and youth. Revs., Providence and Felicity. Good   2 pieces

398 218 A. D. Macrinus. Very fine and sharp portrait. Rev., Health feeding serpent. A very desirable and fine coin

399 222 A. D. Elagabalus. Bearded portrait. Rev., The Emperor officiating as Priest of the Sun (hence his name); a bull at altar; sun above. Very fine

400 222 A. D. Elagabalus. Younger portraits. Revs., Liberty and Fortune. Very good 2 pieces

401 222 A. D. Elagabalus. Revs., "Salus Antonini" and two others. Poor to good 3 pieces.

402 222 A. D. Julia Soaemias. Fine head. Rev., "Venus Caelestis." Fine

403 223 A. D. Julia Maesa. Rev., Pudor seated. Good

404 235 A. D. Alexander Severus. Very fine portrait. Rev., "Jovi Ultori." Very fine

405 235 A. D. Alexander Severus. Fine portraits. Revs., Hope and Equity. Very fine 2 pieces

406 238 A. D. Maximinus I.; and one of Alexander. Rev., Mars Pacifera. Good 2 pieces

407 238 A. D. Pupienus. Radiated head. Rev., Clasped hands of the Emperors. Very good

408 244 A. D. Gordianus III. Various reverses. Good lot 4 pcs

409 249 A. D. Philip II., Valerian, Sr., Gallienus and Postumus. Good 4 pieces

410 267 A. D. Postumus. Fine portrait. Rev., Hercules with club and bow. Fine

ANCIENT BRONZE COINS.

411 44 B. C. Julius Caesar. 1st bronze; head to right. Rev., "Divos Julius" in wreath. Fair

412 23 A. D. Drusus, Jr. 2d bronze. Rev., Large S. C. Also, one of Titus. Good. Latter fair 2 pieces

413 192 A. D. Commodus. 1st bronze. Also, one of Faustina, Jr. Very fair 2 pieces

414 197 A. D. Clodius Albinus. 1st bronze. Rev., Annona seated. Very fair and desirable

415 244 A. D. Gordianus III. 1st bronze; and one of Maximinus I. Both well patinated 2 pieces

416 Lot of 2d, 3d and 4th bronze; various Emperors. A good lot 26 pieces

417 Lot of 2d and 3d bronze; 2 counterfeits. Poor 15 pieces

418 Lot of Byzantine and Bactrian bronze; sizes 12 to 18 11 pcs

419 269 B. C. Hiero II. of Syracuse. Rev., Tridents. Good 2 pcs

420 Egypt. Ptolemaic Dynasty. All different and good; sizes 14 to 19 3 pieces

421 Greek Coins of various cities, &c. Good lot; sizes 7 to 18 25 pieces

1837. TOKENS, ETC.

Catalogued according to Haseltine's Type Table. The closing number
refers to the Lot No. in his catalogue.

422 1834. A plain system void of pomp. L L D on the body
of a balkey donkey. (Does it mean " Long Legged
Devil ?") Uncirculated. 352

423 1834. Hog running, "Perish credit," etc. Uncir. 353

424 1834. Broad-shouldered Jackson. Hog's snout points between H. and C. The best specimen I ever saw. Very
desirable in this condition. 354

425 Jackson in money chest, squares in chest, filled with perfect
lines. Extremely fine. 355

426 Same in brass. Good

427 Same, but lines in chest do not correspond to H or to the
last. Extremely fine. 357

428 Same variety as H. as to lines in squares. Extremely fine.
358.

428a Obv. same. Rev., Ship striking on rock. Extremely fine. 359

429 Obv. nearly the same. Rev., Big-bellied Donkey. Trifle
weak. Uncirculated. 360

430 1837. Turtle. On his back a safe, inscribed " Sub-Treasury." Rev., Donkey running. Extremely fine. 361

431 1837. Same. "Experiment" below instead of "Financer-
ing." Very fine indeed. 362

432 1837. Nearly same variety. Extremely fine. 363

433 1837, '41. Ship ; Eight sail set. "Webster credit," etc.
Fine. 364

434 1837. On rev., 184, no one. Seven sail set. Very good. 365

435 1837, '41. Seven sail set. Current on both sides. Lightning in the sky. Uncirculated. ~~Beautiful piece. Proof
surface.~~

436 1837, '41. Rev., Straight ship, smaller than the last. Very
fine indeed. 367

437 1841. Obv. same. Rev., "Not one cent for Tribute" in
wreath. Uncirculated. Dark. 368

438 1841. Obv. same. Rev., "Not," etc., within circle stars.
Very fine. 369

439 183, 184. The 7 and 1 removed. Same head as the Geo. A. Jarvis card. Rev., Ship; Seven sail set. A leaf before and after " Webster." Not in Type Table. Very fine

440 1837. Phœnix. Rev., Oak wreath, within May Tenth, 1837. Fine. 370

441 1837. Obv., same. Rev., Variety. Fine. 371

442 1837. Obv., same. Rev., in wreath, " Not one," etc. Fine. 372

443 1837. Obv., same. Rev., Variety. Extremely fine. 373

444 1837. Same head as on Devean's card. Rev., " Not," etc. Dark. Very fine indeed. 374

445 1837. Obv., same. Rev., Bentonian Currency. Uncirculated. 375

446 1837. Obv., same. Rev., nearly the same. Fine. 376

447 1837. Obv., same. Rev., " Not," etc., within wreath stars. Very good. 377

448 1837. Obv., same. Rev., Wreath, " Not," etc. Fine to uncirculated. Think there is a slight difference on the revs. 378   2 pieces

449 1837. Obv., same. Rev., May tenth, 1837, within oak wreath. Combination not mentioned by H. Dark. Fine

450 1837. Obv., same. Rev., Center Market. Very good. 380

451 1837. P. B. & S. Devean's card. Obv., same. Rev., Boot. Good. 381

452 1837. Obv., Small head, same as Jarvis' small-headed card. Rev., Within wreath, "Not," etc. Fine. 382

453 1837. Obv., same. Rev., Jarvis' card. Good. 383

454 1837. Head has on it band, inscribed I STICD. Date in large figures. For Tribute, curved more than in any other variety. Better than good. 386

455 1837. Duplicate. Rev., very good. Obv., nearly good

456 1837. *Small* homely head ; *small* date ; *small* " Not"; *small* For Tribute; *small* Millions, etc. Cracked die. It may sell for a *small* price, but in *my opinion* it will not sell *small*. Very good. 387. For Tautology see Bushnell Catalogue

457 1837. Duplicate. " Not " erased. Nearly good

458 1837. If the last head was homely, this is still worse. Two small stars alongside of date. Rev., same. Very good indeed. 388

459 1837. Same head as on Dayton's card. Rev., For Tribute, nearly as much curved as on the United variety. Think it has been cleaned. Fine. 389

460 1837. Obv., same. Rev., J. H. Dayton's card. Obv. fine. 390

461 1837. Same head as on the Maycock and Crossman cards. Rev., "Not one cent" partially obliterated. Barely fair. 392

462 1837. Obv., same. Rev., S. Maycock & Co. Card. Fine. 394

463 1837. Obv., same. Rev., H. Crossman. Card. Very fine. 393

464 1837. Head same as on Jarvis', large headed card. Rev., Not, etc. Good. 396

465 1837. Obv., same. Rev., Geo. A. Jarvis. Card. Perhaps cleaned. Extremely fine. 397

466 1837. Large female head; band inscribed "Liberty." Rev., Ezra B. Sweet's card. Obv., uncirculated. Rev., trifle abused. 398

467 1837. Eagle surrounded by 13 stars; date in exergue. Rev., H. Crossman's card. Fine. 399

468 1837. Same. Rev., S. Maycock's card. Fine. 400

469 1837. Feuchtwanger's composition three cents. Rev., Arms N. Y. Fine. 401

470 1837. Same. Cents. Varieties, fine   3 pieces

471 1838. Ugly head; on band "Locofoco." Rev., Mint drop. Much finer than usual. 402

472 1838. Am I not a woman, etc. Fine. 403

473 1841. Laureated head. Very fine. 404

474 1841. Same. Mint drop. Good. 405

475 1841. Same. Not one, etc. Fine. 406

476 Merchants' Exchange. Rev., same, with the exception of line. Smear. Fine. 407

477 Same. Rev., line under cent. Fine. 408

478 Same, with dome. Rev., No. 6. Tontine, etc. Fine. 409

479 Obv., Abraham Riker's card. Rev., "Not one," etc. Fine. 411

480 Obv., Cow, "A Friend to the Constitution." About fine. 412

2 481 1834-35. Walsh's (2) Clark & Anthony. Richard's cards. Obvs., Lafayette, A friend, etc. Fair to fine 4 pieces
2 482 Various store cards. Same period. Good lot 9 pieces

FOREIGN SILVER COIN.

483 (1272.) England. Edward I. penny. Good
484 (1399.) Same. Henry IV. farthing. Good
485 1580. Same. Elizabeth 2 and 3 pence, 1 pierced. Fair 2 pieces
486 (1558.) Same. Elizabeth shilling. Head weak, otherwise very good indeed
487 (1625.) Same. Charles I. shilling. Fine
488 1684. Same. Charles II. fourpence. Very fine
489 1686. Same. James II. threepence. Black. Good
490 1689. Same. William and Mary fourpence. Good
491 1758, '87. Same. George II. and III. sixpences. Good and uncirculated 2 pieces
492 1804. Same. Bank of England dollar. Very fair
493 1608. Saxony crown (eight dukes). Four busts on each side. Very good. Desirable
494 1684. Carolus II. Neapolitan crown. Bust to right. Rev., American and European hemispheres; between them crown and sceptre. Same as No. 254. Bushnell catalogue, which sold for $19.00. Good and desirable
495 1880. Peru. Cinco Pesetas (dollar). The new issue. Uncir.
496 1880. Same. Una Peseta (quarter). Same. Uncirculated
497 1810, '69, '70. Caracas. 2 real (base). ¼ and ½ Real Honduras Nickel. Very good and fine 3 pieces
498 Tripoli. 10 Piastre (base). Very good
499 Japan. 10, 20 (2) cents. 1st and 2d issues. Good and fine 3 pieces
500 1859. Brazil. 500 Reis, and three other pieces dime size. Fair to uncirculated 4 pieces
501 1864, '66. 5, 10 cents. Maximilian Good 2 pieces
502 Siam. Bullet Money. Eighth tical (8 cents). Very good
503 Japan. ¼ Itzebue. Fine
504 Various. 5 to 15 cent size. Some base 7 pieces

POSTAGE CURRENCY AND CONFEDERATE BILLS.

All in perfect condition unless otherwise stated.

5-5 505 First issue. 25 cents. Perforated edge

2-5 506 Same. 5, 10, 25, 50 cents. Plain edge   4 pieces

3 8 507 Duplicates. 25, 50 cents   2 pieces

2 6 508 Second issue. 5, 10, 25, 50 cents. Only 50 has numerals
           on the back, and is the scarce color   4 pieces

2 3 509 Same. 5, 10, 25, 50 cents. Numerals on back. 5, 25, trifle
           used. 25 on paper that splits   4 pieces

2 8 510 Same. 5, 50 cents. 50 numerals and split paper   2 pieces

/ 2 5- 511 Third issue. 50 cents. Red back. Autographic signatures
           Colby and Spinner. Head of Spinner, but figure 2 on
           back

5-2 512 Same. 50 cents. Head Spinner. Fancy back

5-2 513 Same. 50 cents. Justice seated. Autographic signatures
           Colby and Spinner. Trifle used

5-2 514 Same. 50 cents. Justice. Green back. Numerals

2 6 515 Same. 25 cents. Fessenden. Green back. Trifle used

4 0 516 Same. 10 cents. Washington. Red back. Autographic
           signatures Colby and Spinner

/ 3 517 Same. 10 cents. Washington. Green and red back 2 pcs

/ 8 518 Same. 5 cents. Clark. Green and red back   2 pieces

6 519 Duplicate set   2 pieces

/0' 520 Same. 3 cents. Washington. Dark curtain (2). One
           used, and light curtain   3 pieces

5-2 521 Fourth issue. 50 cents. Head Lincoln

2 6 522 Same. 25 cents. Head Washington

2 0 523 Same. 15 cents. Liberty head. Variety in paper   2 pieces

/ 0 524 Same. 10 cents. Liberty head. Variety in paper   2 pieces

5-5 525 Same. 2d series. 50 cents. Head Stanton

/ 2 526 Fifth issue. 10 cents. Meredith. Red and green seal

5- 527 First issue. 50 cents. Front and two backs separate 2 pcs

/ 0 528 Third issue. 50 cents. Head Spinner. Autographic sig-
           natures Allison and Spinner. Front only

5- 529 Third issue. Fancy green back. Back only

5- 530 Seven backs of 25 cents, and 2 fronts of 50 cents. All
           stamped specimens. 2 are red   9 pieces

4 531 Eight backs of 5 cents. Stamped specimens. 2 are red
           backs   8 pieces

532 1861. July 25. Ten dollars. Confederate. Fem de leau
    ing on shield. Eagle to right. Very good

533 1861. Same. 5 dollars. Same to left. Sailor leaning on
    capstan. Very good

534 1861. September 2. Twenty dollars. 3 females seated to
    left. Liberty standing. Green front. Good

535 1861. Same. 10 dollars. Load of cotton in centre. Good

536 1861. Same. Same. Indians seated in centre. Printed
    by Southern Bank Note Co. Good

537 1861. Same. Same. Female leaning on anchor. Fine

538 1861. Same. 5 dollars. Blacksmith seated to right. Good

539 1861. Same. 50 dollars. Female seated by money chest.
    Fine

540 1861. Sept. 23. 100 dollars. Train cars in centre. Printed
    by Southern Bank Note Co. Beautiful piece

541 1862, '4. Two dollars (2). 10 dollars. Fine. 3 pieces

PATTERNS, Etc.

All Silver unless otherwise stated.

542 1838. Half dollar. Flying eagle. Carried as a pocket
    piece, and abused. Pierced. Very fair

543 1858. Oak wreath. Cent. Extremely fine

544 1859. ½ dollar. Copper proof

545 1859. 50 cents. Copper proof

546 1859. Half dollar. Copper proof

547 1860. Five dollars. French head. Brilliant copper proof

548 1861. Clark, Gruber & Co. 5, 10, 20 dollars. Tin proofs.
    1 misstruck   3 pieces

549 1863. Head Washington. Two cent piece. Copper. Bril-
    liant proof

550 1863. Postage currency. Lead. Fair

551 1865. Dollar. "In God we Trust." Copper. Brilliant
    proof

552 1865. Half dollar. Same motto. Copper. Brilliant proof

553 1865. Quarter dollar. Same. Copper. Brilliant proof

554 1865. Two cent piece. Obv., Copper. Rev., Silver. Bril-
    liant proof. Desirable

— *0* 555 1867. 5 Cents. Nickel. 5 cents in wreath. Brilliant proof

o J 556 1867. Same. Aluminum. Large V over shield. Brilliant proof

o⁻J⁻0 557 1869. Halves, quarters, and dimes, the three varieties. Mint price was $15. Splendid proofs   9 pieces

3o 558 1869. Varieties of half dollars. Copper proofs   3 pieces

⸍ ꝗ 7ɔ⁻ 559 1870. Longacre dollar. Indian Queen seated on a globe. Band on it inscribed Liberty. Liberty cap, flags, etc. Rev., Same as regular dollar. Brilliant proof. Very desirable

Z 7ɔ 560 1873. Dollar. One of the pattern set of six. The type with the obv. like the regular trade dollar. Brilliant proof. Desirable

J⁻J⁻Z 561 1878. Goloid metric 100 cents. 1—G. 16.1—S. 1.9—C. Grams 14.25. Brilliant proof. Only 25 struck. Desirable

J⁻2 ɔ⁻ 562 1878. Morgan design for the dollar. On rev., the branch in eagle's claw has only one leaf. Beautiful proof. Desirable

ꝗ 7ɔ⁻ 563 1879. Goloid metric dollar. 100 cents. 15.3—G. 236.7 —S. 28—C. 14 Grams. Deo est gloria. Obv., Head. E pluribus unum above. Brilliant proof. Desirable

⸍ 564 1803. Kettle. Half and quarter eagle. 2 pierced. Fair to good. Copper and gilt   9 pieces

INDIAN IMPLEMENTS OF THE STONE AGE.

2 0 565 Grooved axe, 7 in. long by 3½ in. wide ; broken edge, but not injuring the form much

Z J 566 Grooved hatchet, 4 in. long by 2 in. wide. Very good

⸍ J⁻ 567 Grooved hatchet, 3½ in. long by 2½ wide. Very fair

⸍ . 568 Skin dresser or Peeler, 4½ in. long. Good

0 569 Skin dresser, 2¾ in. long. Fine specimen

⸍ . 570 Spearhead. Fine and symmetrical. Slight defect on haft. 4¼ in. long

⸍ . 571 Spearheads. Flint and slate ; latter defective on one edge, otherwise of fine proportions. 4¼ long x 3 wide. Good
                                                 2 pieces

⸍ . 572 Spearheads. Light and dark flint ; all different forms. 3 to 4 in. long. Fine   4 pieces

573 Spearheads. Light quartz and flint; different forms. 2 to 3¼ in. long   Good   4 pieces

574 Spearheads, defective. One a soft red clay stone. 3 and 5 in. long   2 pieces

575 Arrowheads. Fine lot of various colors. From 1 to 2½ in. long. A very desirable lot   27 pieces

576 Arrowheads. Principally quartz. 1 to 1½ in. long. Good lot   35 pieces

577 Arrowheads. Quartz, jasper and flint. Smaller than last lot. Good   30 pieces

MISCELLANEOUS.

578 U. S. revenue stamps. No duplicates   70 pieces

579 Duplicate revenue stamps. Some foreign   100 pieces

580 Uncancelled postage stamps, foreign, including a 5c. N. Y. P. O. Not all different   50 pieces

581 Cancelled postage stamps. Foreign and domestic. About 1500. Sold as a lot

582 Permanent postage stamp Album. 1876. Unused

583 Collection of minerals. 50 specimens. All named

584 Thomas' Almanacs for 1802-'03-'04-'13 '17-'22 '25 '27-'50 -'52-'53-'54-'58-'59-'60 and '62. A good line   16 pieces

585 Old Almanacs for 1822, '49, '54, '58, '67 and '72   6 pieces

586 Old Newspapers: "Boston Gazette," 1774; "Conn. Courant," 1774, and "True American," 1798 (damaged). 5 pcs.

587 Penna. Packet, 1775; fine   3 pieces

588 Correspondence between Citizen Genet, of France, and the U. S. Officials. Printed by B. F. Bache, 1793. Fine, desirable

589 Reprints: Amateur and Know-Nothing Papers   15 pcs.

590 New Orleans Delta, 1862; Era, 1864; Mobile Tribune, 1867. Interesting rebellion news. 2 duplicates   5 pcs.

591 1856. Barometric Reports for 1856. Large 4to vol. with charts

592 Scrap-Book of Clippings, &c., relating to the Rebellion

593 De Sauley. Numismatique Judaique. Paris, 1854. Fine copy. Half morocco, 4to

594 Dickeson's Manual. Cloth, 4to   Phil. 1859

595 Jones' Coin Collector's Manual. Cloth, 4to   Phil. 1860

ᴐ '₂ 596 Crosby's Early Coins of America. 12 Nos., unbound
7ᴜ 597 Maris' varieties of 1794 cents, 1869
2ᴣ⁻ 598 Haseltine's Colonial and Continental Paper Money. Illustrated. 1872
ᴣ⁻ 599 Coin Collector's Guide, 1880. Nos. 1, 2 and 3   3 pieces
ᴜ 600 Magic duplicating and impression paper. 12 packages. 4 colors in each. Sold as a lot
/ᴣ⁻ 601 Haseltine.   Type Table Catalogue.   Unpriced
ᴣ⁻ 602 Haseltine.   Coin sales, 1875 to '79.   All priced.   9 pieces
ᴣ⁻ 603 Cogan.   April and September, 1863 ; April, 1867, and Nov. '74.   All priced   4 pieces
// 604 Steigerwalt,   Feb. and June, '81.   Priced   2 pieces
/ᴑ 605 Woodward,   Oct., 1863 ; Haines, Jan., '63.   Priced   2 pcs.
ᴣ 606 Mason,   Oct., 69 ; Bangs, Feb., '62 ; Birch, June, '71 ; Scott, Oct., '79.   All priced   4 pieces
ᴣᴑ 607 Maranville's Pocket Coin Tester. Brass, with directions
ᴣ‾ᴜ 608 Coin Cabinet.   Black walnut ; 14¼ in. high, 16 wide, and 9 in. deep ; 12 drawers

SILVER AND BASE-MONEY PROOF SETS.

7ᴜ 609 1861.   Splendid proof set   7 pieces
ᴣᴣᴑ 610 1870.   Brilliant set   10 pieces
ᴣ‾ᴜ 611 1872.   Brilliant proofs   10 pieces
4/ᴜ 612 1872.   Beautiful proofs   10 pieces
ᴣ‾2ᴑ 613 1873.   Old style. Beautiful proofs   10 pieces
ᴣ‾ᴜ 614 1873.   Same. Brilliant proofs   10 pieces
ᴣ‾ᴜ 615 1873.   Trade set. Brilliant proofs   7 pieces
ᴣ‾ᴜ 616 1873.   Duplicate set   7 pieces
ᴌ ᴣᴜ 617 1878.   Brilliant proofs.   20 cent piece, but no Bland dollar   7 pieces
ᴣ‾ᴜ 618 1879.   Beautiful proofs. Both dollars   8 pieces
ᴣ‾ᴜ 619 1880.   Splendid set. Both dollars   8 pieces
ᴣᴣ‾620 1869.   Base money. Splendid proofs   4 pieces
ᴣᴣ⁻ 621 1869.   Splendid proofs   4 pieces
4ᴌ 622 1871.   Brilliant proofs   4 pieces
4ᴑ 623 1871.   Duplicate set   4 pieces
ᴌ/ 624 1871.   Another set   4 pieces
ᴣ⁻ 625 1872.   Brilliant proofs   4 pieces
/ᴌᴌ 626 1873.   Brilliant proofs   4 pieces

627 1874. Brilliant proofs   3 pieces
628 1875. Brilliant proofs   2 sets
629 1876. Brilliant proofs   3 pieces
630 1878. Brilliant proofs   2 sets
631 1879. Brilliant proofs   3 pieces
632 1879. Duplicate set   3 pieces
633 1880. Beautiful proofs   3 pieces
634 1880. Duplicates   2 sets
635 1881. Beautiful proofs   3 pieces
636 1881. Duplicates   2 sets
637 1881. More of them   2 sets
638 1882. Splendid proofs   3 pieces
639 1882. Duplicates   2 sets
640 1873. Two cent piece. Brilliant proof
641 1873. Same. Brilliant proof
642 1873. Same. Proof. Has been in circulation
643 1877. 5 cent nickel. Brilliant proof

QUARTER DOLLARS, Etc.

644 1815. QUARTER. Nicked. Very fair indeed
645 1815. Fair. 1 pierced   5 pieces
646 1819. Fine. Desirable in this condition
647 1805, '6 (2). '7, '15, '18, '19 (2), '22, '24, '28. Fair to
    very good   11 pieces
648 1831. Very good
649 1853, '56. Very fine. Some lustre   2 pieces
650 1857. Uncirculated. Lustre
651 1859. Brilliant proof
652 1861. Uncirculated. Lustre
653 1862. Brilliant proof
654 1865. Extremely fine. Lustre
655 1871. Uncirculated and very sharp. Lustre
656 1879. Uncirculated. Brilliant lustre
657 1881. Uncirculated. Lustre
658 1875. TWENTY CENTS. San Francisco. Extremely fine
    2 pieces
659 1875. Same mint. Same   2 pieces
660 1875. Uncirculated. Lustre   2 pieces
661 1876. Fine and extremely fine   2 pieces

662 1796. DIME. Very good for date
663 1805. Good impression
664 1805, '7, '11. Fair to very fair   3 pieces
665 1822. Worn. Fair and desirable
666 1822. Five cuts on obv. Fair
667 1814, '20, '21 (2), '23. Fair to good   5 pieces
668 1824. Over 23. Very fair indeed. Desirable
669 1827. Nicked. Fine impression
670 1827, '28 Small, '33, '34, '35 (2), 36. Very good to very fine
                                   7 pieces
671 1837. Head and Liberty seated. Very fine lot   4 pieces
672 1838. N. O., without stars. Very good and desirable
673 1838. Stars. Very fine indeed. Lustre   2 pieces
674 1839. Extremely fine. Lustre·
675 1838, '39 (3). Very fine to extremely fine. Lustre. 4 pieces
676 1840. Draped and undraped. Fair to extremely fine 3 pes
677 1844 (2), '45. Good to very fine   3 pieces
678 1846. Very good. Desirable
679 1846. Good. Desirable
680 1846. About the same.
681 1853. No arrows, '56. Large and small. Good   4 pieces
682 1857. N. O., 58. Very good to extremely fine   2 pieces
683 1860. San Francisco. Stars. Nearly good
684 1862. Brilliant proof
685 1869, '70, '71. Very fine.   3 pieces
686 1873. No arrows. Brilliant proof
687 1873. Same. Very fine indeed. Lustre   4 pieces
688 1874. Uncirculated. Lustre   2 pieces
689 1874. Duplicates. Same   2 pieces
690 1874. Same in all respects   2 pieces
691 1876, '78. Proof and very fine   2 pieces
692 1879. Uncirculated. Lustre
693 1795. HALF DIME. Indented. Good
694 1795. Cracked die, pierced at side. About good
695 1800. Very fair ; desirable
696 1800. Barely fair. Date plain. Rev. poor
697 1829. Good to fine   3 pieces
698 1837, '38 (3). No stars. '40, both '41, '42 (2). Fair to fine
                                   9 pieces
699 1844 (4), '45 (2). Very fair to good   7 pieces

700 1847, '49. Fine impression   2 pieces

701 1850-'57. Includes some duplicates. Good to uncirculated   20 pieces

702 1858 (2), '59 (3). Fine to uncirculated. 1 N. O.   5 pieces

703 1860 (2), '61, '62 (5). Extremely fine to uncirculated. Lustre   8 pieces

704 1863. Fine impression

705 1870 (4), '71 (3), '72 (2). Very fine to uncirculated. 9 pieces

706 1873. Brilliant proofs   4 pieces

707 1873. Brilliant proofs   4 pieces

708 1873. Brilliant proofs   4 pieces

709 1873. Duplicates   4 pieces

710 1851 (2), '2, '3, '4, '5, '6, '7, '9, '60, '1. THREE CENTS, silver. Very good   6 pieces

711 Same. Very good to uncirculated   5 pieces

712 1855. Nicked. Fine

713 1855. Same condition

714 1855. About the same

715 1855. Very good   2 pieces

716 1855. Nearly the same   2 pieces

717 1858. Brilliant proof. Desirable

718 1858. Brilliant proof. Desirable

719 1862. Brilliant proof

720 1863. Brilliant proof

721 1865. Uncirculated. Lustre

722 1866. Brilliant proof

723 1866. Brilliant proof

724 1867. Brilliant proof

725 1868. Brilliant proof

726 1869. Brilliant proof

727 1870. Brilliant proof

728 1872. Brilliant proof

729 1873. Brilliant proof. Desirable

730 1873. Brilliant proof. In demand

MEDALS, MASONIC, &c.

ALL FINE, UNLESS OTHERWISE STATED.

731 Electrotype of the Gen. Meade medal; in appearance equal to an original; copper bronzed. Size 50

732 Electrotype of Thomas Jefferson peace medal. Zinc bronzed. Size 47

733 Wm. H. Seward. Very fine portrait in alto-relievo ; struck in France. A hard composition like gutta percha. Size 70

734 Cyrus W. Field. Rev., "Nil desperandum." Cracked die. Bronze. Size 32

735 New Jersey Agr. Soc. ; awarded for equestrianism. Silver. Size 36

736 War medal given by N. Y. City to Soldiers in Mexican War. Has been plugged. Nearly fine. Silver. Size 33

737 Victoria war medal, clasp Taku Forts, 1860, "For long service," etc. Silver. 23

738 Stonewall Jackson. In case. White metal. 32

739 Dr. Baron Decanus. Bust to right. Rev., Storks on shield; "Facult. Medic. Paris, 1754." Bronze. Size 18

740 Dr. Winslow Lewis, M. D. Bust to left. Copper. Size 20

741 1732. Laura M. C. Bassi, Ph. D. Bust in high relief. Rev., Minerva, with lamp, advancing to female on right; owl on globe. Bronze. Size 44

742 Queen Christina of Sweden. Fine bust to right. Rev., The constellation Leo with orb, rudder and cornucopia. Bronze. Size 39

N. B.—The foregoing two medals were struck on planchets previously cast, to facilitate sharp striking, as is often the case with even modern medals. I make this explanation for collectors unacquainted with the process of manufacturing medals, who are unaware that it often requires from five to twenty-five blows from a heavy press to make a clear impression.

743 Martin Luther. Bust to left. Rev., A heart in centre of a rose. An old cast silver medal, unlike any I've seen (but not necessarily unique). Good. Size 25

744 1858. New Orleans Mutual Benefit Society. Silver. Size 15. Good. And Boston Numismatic Soc. Copper. 20 2 pieces

745 1852. St. Matthaeus Church, N.Y. (Lutheran); Odd Fellows' Hall, Centre St., and 8th St. Turner-Halle medals. White medals. Good. Size 20 to 24 3 pieces

746 1784. Phila. Museum. Bust of Peale. Very good. Copper. 20

747 1880. 150th Aniversary (sic) of founding of Baltimore. Obv., Bust of Calvert. Bronze or "oreide." Size 20

748 Pius IX., Dr. Tyng, Buckalew, and Sallust. Copper and
white metal. Sizes 18 to 21. 4 pieces

749 Union League (3 kinds) and three other medals. Copper
and brass. 12 to 23 6 pieces

750 1881. G. A. R. encampment at Pittsburgh. Silver shield
medal, with clasp; sizes 14 to 20; and 1879, Gen. E. D.
Baker. Rev., Post 8, Phila. Bronze. Size 12 2 pieces

751 1876. St. Albans Com. K. T. Centennial shield. Nickel
plated. 24 x 32

752 5873. Phila. Masonic Temple, and N. Y. Temple, 1875.
Shield-shaped. White metal and brass. Sizes 24 and 32.
3 pieces

753 5876. Masons of Europe to U. S. Brethren. Obv., Radiated
G in emblems. Gilt bronze. 24

754 Long's masonic card, in silver. Size 18.

755 Long's card, in copper. White metal medal. Obv., Keystone,
and gilt Washington. Rev., Emblems on book. Sizes 12
to 18 3 pieces

756 1863. Wood and Johnston's masonic cards. Good 2 pieces

757 1795. Masonic ½d. Obv., Bust of Fred., Duke York;
" London and Dublin " on edge

758 1790. Masonic ½d. Usual type, but " Payable at the Black
Horse, Tower Hill," on edge

759 5804. Triple Unite Ecossaise O. de Paris. Rev., Emblems
within endless serpent. Bronze. Size 18

760 A. Bildung V. Square and compasses. Rev., Large star in
circle of 16 stars. Brass. Very fair. Never saw it before. Size 14

761 1810. Orphelines de la Légion d'Honneur. Rev., Wreath.
Bronze. Size 26

762 1876. Veyrat's Centennial medal. Helmeted head to left.
Rev., Crossed U. S. flags. A beautiful bronze. Size 25

763 1876. Centennial Commission. Unlovely Liberty in an
uncomfortable position. Bronze in case. Size 36

764 1876. Same as last, but beautified with gilt. Size 36.

764a 1876. Small medal, with similar obv.; bronze; also, the
fine Lexington medal in white metal, unpierced. Size 24.
2 pieces

765 1876. Centennial production of Nevada ore. Rev., Long,
but one legged soldiers, presenting marvellous arms. Silver. 24

3 766 Copenhagen Centennial. " Let us have peace;" also, one of
        main building; white metal. Sizes 26 and 33   2 pieces
4 767 Centennials. Ind. Hall. Statue in front. Bronze and white
        metal; "International," brass; and, "July 5th," in white
        metal. Sizes 15 to 24   4 pieces
10 768 Politicals. Hayes, Tilden, Grant, Greeley, etc. White
        metal, copper, brass, nickel and rubber   16 pieces
4 769 Buck, Cannon and Breckinridge ; Fremont and Harrison; 3
        pierced. White metal and brass. Sizes 15 to 29   5 pcs
5 770 Lincolns, by Key and Lovett. Silver, copper, brass and
        white metal. 16 to 26   7 pieces
3 771 Grant. Copper, white metal and rubber. Good. 12 to
        20   7 pieces
30 772 Garfield to left. Barber's untruthful portrait. Rev., Lincoln,
        Silver. Issued at the Mint. Size 16
11 773 Garfield. Rev., " Civic Wreath." Rev., canal scene, and
        the Satanic figure. Bronze and white metal. 16 to 24
                                                        3 pieces
2,2 774 Garfield and Hancock Medals. 2 kinds, gilt. Size 16
                                                        24 pieces
2 775 Hancock Badges (one Satanical) and Seymour and Blair
        Buttons   5 pieces
2 1/4 776 Washington. Tokens, Cards, &c. Various metals. Sizes
        12 to 20   19 pieces
2 777 Washington Medals, 1848. National Monument (which Mr.
        Haseltine says is scarce). Robinson's, Merriam's, Curtis',
        Dickeson's and Bales' Medals. White metal, copper
        nickel and silver. Sizes 11 to 25   7 pieces
30 778 Westwood's " George Washington, Esq." Rev., "Made
        Commander," etc. Bronze. Very good. Size 25
25 779 Washington. Old bust to right, " George Washington, ob.
        14 Dec., 1799, ae. 68." Bronze. Very good. Size 24
15 780 Manly's Washington. S. B. F. on shoulder; 11 Feb., O. S.,
        1732 below. Re-strike bronze. Size 30
3 781 Wyon's Washington, 1796. Bust to right. Rev., "Repub.
        Ameri." on scroll over caduceus, fasces and cannon.
        Bronze. Size 21
   782 Lovett's Heavy-jawed Washington. Rev., Jap. Embassy.
        Bronze. Size 34
   783 1859. Medallic Steel Engraving of Washington, covered by
        glass and framed with Mt. Vernon wood. Size 50

784 Central America. Bronze idol, cast and rude, but not guaranteed antique. 2 inches high

785 Egypt. Ancient bronze idol of Osiris. Has been in fire. Good. 4 inches high

786 Egypt. Clay mummy. Unglazed. Fair. 2½ inches high

787 Egypt. Antique Scarabeii. Clay and terra-vert. All chipped, but genuine 4 pieces

COLONIALS AND 1837 TOKENS.

788 1652. Pine tree shilling; ten branches to tree, small planchet-indented. Good

789 1788. Massachusetts Cent. Obv., good. Rev., fair

790 1788. Massachusetts Half Cent. Rev. has been trifle corroded. Dark, sharp, desirable

791 1787. Immunis Columbia. Minute blemish on edge barely perceptible. Dark, fine, desirable

792 1787. Vermon Auctori. Rev., Inde et Lib. Planchet defective at Rmon. Olive. About fine

793 Vermonts Res Publica. Planchet trifle defective. Very fair. Desirable

794 Vermontis Res Publica. Very fair. Desirable

795 1723. Wood Halfpenny, indented, 1724. Farthing and Columbia Farthing, 1 cleaned. Good 3 pieces

796 Connecticut, New York, Vermont and other colonials. Poor to good 54 pieces

Closing number refers to Haseltine's Type Table.

797 1834. Plain System Void of Pomp. Fine. 352

798 1834. Hog running. "Perish Credit," etc. Very fine. 353

799 1834. Same. Broad-shouldered Jackson. Fine. 354

800 Jackson in Money Chest. Extremely fine. 355

801 Same. Squares not all full. Brass plated. Fine. 356

802 Same. Olive. Fine. 2 pieces. 357

803 1837. Same obv. Rev., ship striking rocks. Very fine. 359

404 Similar obv. Rev., Big-bellied donkey. Very fine. 360

805 1837. Turtle with safe. About fine. 2 pieces. 361 2

806 1837-41. Same. Very fine indeed. 363

807 1837-41. Ship's 7 and 8 sail. Good. 2 pieces. 364 5

808 1837-41. Ship's 7 sail. Rev., Lightning. Good. 366

809 1837–41. Same. Rev., Curved ship, lightning. Uncirculated. 367

810 1837–41. Obv. same. Rev., Not, etc. Cleaned. Good. 368

811 1837. Obv. same. Rev., Circle stars. Very fine. 369

812 1837. Phœnix. The 4 varieties. Good. 4 pieces. 370–1–2–3

813 1837. Deveau Head. 7 varieties. Good. 7 pieces. 374 to 380

814 1837. Jarvis small Head. Good. 382

815 1837. Obv. same. Rev., Center Market. 384

816 1837. Obv. same. Rev. not in H. Fair

817 1837. United head. Edge of planchet trifle abused. Very good indeed. 386

818 1837. Ugly head. 2 small stars at side of dates. Indented. Otherwise about good. 388

819 1837. Female head. "Not," scratched out. Very fair. Desirable variety. 389

820 1837. Feuchtwanger 3 cent piece. Arms of New York. Very fine. 401

821 1837. Same. Cent. Extremely fine

822 1837. Half-cents worth, &c. Very fine. Desirable

823 1838. "Locofoco" head. Rev., Mint drop. Extremely fine. 402

824 1838. Am I not a woman, &c. Cleaned. Very fine. 403

825 1841. The 3 varieties. Good. 404, 5, 6

826 Merchants' Exchange, with steeple. Dash and no dash under cent. Good and very fine. 2 pieces. 407, 8

827 Same. With dome. Rev., Tontine Building. Sharply struck. Extremely fine. 409

828 Abraham Riker's card. Boot, shoe, &c. Rev., Not one, &c. Without dash under cent. Very fine indeed. Not in H.

829 Obv. A cow. Friend to the Constitution. Rev., Ship, agriculture, &c. Fine. 412

830 1837. Both varieties of heads. Rev. George A. Jarvis' store cards. Very good   2 pieces

831 1837. Both varieties of H. Crossman's store card, and one of S. Maycock & Co. Fine   3 pieces

832 Various store cards. Deveau's, Sweet, &c. Fair to good   12 pieces

U. S. SILVER DOLLARS.

1795. Flowing hair. Planchet trifle rough on obv. Sharp, strong impression. Barely circulated. Desirable

1795. Same. Very good impression

1795. A few trifling scratches on the obv. In some respects a better impression than the last lot

1795. Edge trifle nicked. Scratched on obv. Very fair

1795. Fillet head. Rev., Edge of planchet cracked; cut extending to wreath. Nearly good

1795. Same. Nicked. Very fair

1795. Same. File marks on bust and edge of planchet. Good

1796. Small date. Large letters on rev. Good

1796. Same Small letters on rev. Edge in one place not perfect. Very good

1797. Six stars facing. Obv., Two light cuts across the planchet. Nick on rev. Fine

1797. Same. Obv. planchet rough. Rev. little weak. Very good

1797. Same. Obv. blurred appearance. Rev. weak and scratches. Very fair

1798. Large eagle. Broken die back of bust. Blurred look of two stars and LIB Very good

1798. Same. 8 touches bust. Good

1798. Same. 8 away from bust. About fine

1798. Same. Stars weak. Back of bust. Nearly good

1798. Same variety as last lot. Somewhat better

1798. Rev. trifling scratch. Obv. slight scrape. Good

1798. Same. Nicked. About good

1798. Same. Weak in one place on rev. Nicked. Fine

1798. Same. Nicked. Fine

1798. Same. Rev. cut from wing into stars. Nicked. Very good

1798. Same. Weak spot on rev. in stars and one cloud. Very good

1798. Same. Minute file marks on bust. About fine

1798. Same. Nicked. Fine

1798. Break in die back of bust. Fine

1798. Stars weak on rev. Obv., die cracked. About good

	860	1798.	Very fair, indeed
2 0	861	1798.	A good impression
	862	1798.	Obv., cracked die. Good
	863	1798.	Nicked. Fine
1 , 0	864	1799 over '98. Nicked. Rev., broken die, through I in America. Good
	865	1799 over '98. Nicked. Nearly good
1 2 6	866	1799.	Very fine impression
1 5	867	1799.	Trifling break in planchet on edge. Very fine
1 5	868	1799.	Fine and very fine. 2 pieces
1 3 2	869	1799.	Fine and very fine, indeed. 2 pieces
1 5	870	1799.	One planchet on edge trifle defective. Very fine and fine. 2 pieces
2 2	871	1799.	Very good, indeed. 2 pieces
	872	1799.	Good and fine. 2 pieces
	873	1799.	Same condition. 2 pieces
	874	1799.	One scratched on rev. Very good. 2 pieces
	875	1799.	Very good impression. 2 pieces
1 1 0	876	1799.	Very good, indeed. 2 pieces
	877	1799.	Good and very good. 2 pieces
	878	1799.	Good and fine. 2 pieces
	879	1799.	One, edge trifle abused. Fine. 2 pieces
	880	1799.	One, edge minute defect. Good and very good. 2 pcs.
	881	1799.	One, stars weak on rev. Same condition. 2 pieces
	882	1799.	Fair to very good. 3 pieces
2 0 0	883	1800.	Comet variety. Very fine. Desirable
1 3 0	884	1800.	Edge trifle nicked. Very good
1 2 0	885	1800.	Very fair impression
1 2 5	886	1800.	Good impression
1 2 0	887	1800.	Indented. Very fair
1 4 0	888	1801.	Nicked. Very fair
1 6 0	889	1802 over 1. Nicked. Very good
1 3 5	890	1802 over 1. Variety. Nicked. Good
1 6 0	891	1802.	Very good, indeed
1 6 0	892	1803.	Large 3. Obv., fine ; rev., good
1 3 5	893	1803.	Small 3. Scratched on obv. Nearly good
1 0 5	894	1843.	Nicked. Fine
0 5	895	1844.	Nicked. Good
1 0 5	896	1853.	Very fair
1 5	897	1853.	Same condition
5	898	1855.	Good impression for date

HALF DOLLARS.

899 1795. Double date. Originally cut near the border; afterwards recut higher up. Good and desirable
900 1795. Trifling file marks on bust. Nicked. Good
901 1795. About the same condition
902 1795. Nearly good. 2 pieces
903 1795. About the same. 2 pieces
904 1795. Trifling scratches. Very fair. 2 pieces
905 1801. Very fair. Edge trifle abused
906 1801. Somewhat better
907 1803. Small crooked 3. About fine
908 1803. Large 3. Very good. 2 pieces
909 1803. Nearly fine. 2 pieces
910 1803. Good impressions. 2 pieces
911 1803. Nearly same. 2 pieces
912 1805. Trifling scratches. Good. 2 pieces
913 1805. Nearly same condition. 2 pieces
914 1806. Blunt 6. Nearly good. 2 pieces
915 1806. Same. Nearly same condition. 3 pieces
916 1807. Head facing right. Fine
917 1815. Very good. Desirable
918 1815. Good impression. Desirable
919 1818 over 17. Spread 8. Fine
920 1824. Close date. Uncirculated. Lustre
921 1825. Very fine, indeed
922 1828. Large date. Curled 2. Fine
923 1861. Scott's restrike of the Confederate half dollar. A fine impression. Desirable

AMERICAN GOLD, Etc.

924 1797. Ten dollars. Stars all sharp. Fine polished surface. Extremely fine. Desirable.
925 1797. Ten dollars. Variety. Good
926 1801. Ten dollars. Polished surface. Very fine indeed
927 1803. Ten dollars. Crooked 3. Small stars on rev.; also one or two file marks. Very fine indeed
928 1798. Half eagle. Nicked. Very fine

7 3θ 929 1800. Half eagle. Polished surface. Extremely fine

5-5-5 930 1806. Half eagle. Blunt 6. Very fine

-5-5- 931 1807. Half eagle. Head right. Nicked a trifle. Very
fine

6 5θ 932 1807. Half eagle. Head left. Very fine

5-55- 933 1810. Half eagle. Very fine

5-3θ 934 1818. Half eagle. Head nicked and small cut on it. Otherwise fine

7θ0 935 1836. Half eagle. Brilliant. Extremely fine

7θ5 936 1802. Quarter eagle. Obv., Minute nick. Rev., Eagle
and clouds, show trifling file marks. Very fine and desirable

5 55- 937 1804. Quarter eagle. File marks show on cap and on
edge. Lustre. Extremely fine and desirable

4 75- 938 1808. Quarter eagle. Minute blemish before date. Very
fine and desirable

2 70 939 1835. Quarter eagle. Pin scratches in field. Polished
surface. Extremely fine

4 θ7 940 1836. Quarter eagle. Very fine indeed

3 10 941 1874. Three-dollar piece. Nicked. Very fine

6 25- 942 Five dollars. C. Bechtler, At Rutherf. Rev., Georgia
gold, 128 G., 22 carats. Very good

7θ 943 1850. G. S. L. C. P. G. Five dollars. Rev., "*To the
Lord Holiness.*" Stars. Mormon cap. All Seeing Eye.
About fine. Very desirable

2 10 944 One dol. A. Bechtler. Carolina gold, 27 G., 21 C. Extremely fine

17 75- 945 1861. Confederate States of America. Bust of Liberty.
Rev., Wreath made up of corn, rice, tobacco leaves,
whiskey and turpentine barrels, bale cotton, etc., within
one cent. Brilliant proof. It is said to be a positive
fact that only seven of these pieces are in existence. Desirable

946 1879. One Stella, 400 cents. Pattern Four-dollar gold
piece of the U. S.

Recommended by committee of coinage, weights and measures,
that it be adopted by the Government for the supposititious
reason, that as four dollars is the pound of Newfoundland, the
good people of this country want a handy money to buy codfish
with. The piece is a brilliant proof and desirable.

2 _ 917 Byzantine. Soldus. Johann II. Comenus. Pierced. Very
fair

7 918 Byzantine. Half soldus. Johann II. Pierced. Very fair

FOREIGN SILVER COIN.

9 9 9 919 (1578.) Crown. Doge Nicholaus Depoute. A cross.
Rev., Lion of St. Mark on shield. Fine

4 - 950 1632. Crown, of Gustavus Adolphus. Bust ¼ face. Rev.,
arms of Sweden and Finland, arms of Augsburg below.
Very fine. Desirable

4 951 1680. Leopold the Hog Mouth. *Box Crown*, made to carry
secret despatches. Very fine and desirable

2 9 9 952 1682. Crown of Salzburg. Two bishops standing. Rev.,
Saints Martin, Vincent, etc. Uncirculated. Desirable

2 82 953 1781. Crown. Eichstadt. Sede Vacante. Two Saints
on clouds above the city; eye in radiated triangle. Rev.,
Sixteen shield of arms. Polished surface. Uncirculated

3 0 954 1767. Hesse. ⅔ crown. Frederick 2d. Bust to right.
Rev., Crowned lions supporting shield with the Garter
motto. Uncirculated

5 ee 955 1746. Russia. Rouble of Elizabeth the I. Extensively
developed bust of Empress. Rev., Imperial eagle. Very
fine impression

- 956 1762. Russia. Rouble of Peter III. Mailed bust to right.
Rev., Arms. Uncirculated. Splendid impression

2 957 1796. Hesse-Hanau. Crown of William IX. Large head
to right. Rev., Order of the Seraphim beneath arms.
Very find

2 958 1796. Salzburg. Crown. Bust of Cardinal Jerome. Rev.,
Arms, backed by a fur mantle. Beautiful uncirculated piece

5 959 1745. Crown of Francis I. of Germany. Rev., Fine view
of the City of Nuremburg. "Tuta His Auspiciis."
Scratch in field, otherwise fine

960 1800. Rome. Crown. Pius VII. Obv., Papal arms.
Rev., Religon seated amid clouds. Good

961 1848. Venice. 5 lire, struck during the siege of that city
under Daniele Manin. Lion on a pedestal. Very good.
Historical

6 2 **962** 1832. Baden. Crown of Leopold. Head to right. Rev., Arms supported by griffons. Very fine

45 **963** 1802. Cis-Alpine Republic. 30 soldi, struck in honor of Bonaparte. Very good

70 **964** 1255. A. H. Turkey. 20 piastre. Good

1 35 **965** 1804. Geo. III. Bank of England dollar. Very good

1 25 **966** 1871. Honduras. 50 centavos. Obv., Crowned arms backed by flags. Rev., Tree in wreath. Fine. Desirable

3 35 **967** 1871. Honduras. 25 centavos. Same design as last. Fine

90 **968** 1872. Bolivian dollar. 9 stars beneath arms. Good

70 **969** 1880. Peru. Dollar. The new design of the head of Liberty, by Bovy. Rev., Radiated oak wreath above arms. Uncirculated

50 **970** 1829. Haiti. Boyer An. 26. 100 centime piece (or, quoting the authorities of the Bushnell catalogue, "100 cents or dollar"). This piece is genuine. Nearly good, and not in the least rare

170 **971** 1881. Haiti. Gourde (Dollar). 900 fine. Beautiful head to right, by *Laforesterie*. Rev., The Haitian national arms, one of the handsomest modern coins, also 20 and 10 cent pieces of the same design reduced. Uncirculated. The first set of this kind ever offered for sale. 3 pieces

75 **972** 1881. Another set, same as last in every particular. 3 pcs.

30 **973** 1881. 20 and 10 cent pieces, same as last. Uncir. 2 pcs.

25 **974** 1881. Another 10 and 20 cent. Same as last. Unc. 2 pcs.

250 **975** 1879. Goloid Patterns of the United States, including the Stella four dollar gold piece. Also the two single dollars. Very desirable. Brilliant proofs 3 pieces

150 **976** 1877. Uruguay Dollar. Obv., Arms, flags, cannon, etc.; rev., "Libre y constituida, 1 Peso"; I believe the first offered at auction. Fine

5 **977** 1865. Bolivia. Dollar of Gen. Melgarejo; his bust to left. Rev., "Gratitude of Potosi." Very good

90 **978** 1868. Bolivia. Real of Melgarejo; his bust to left; "The great citizen of Bolivia." Rev., Open book, "a la constitution de 1868." Fine

5 **979** 1829. Bolivia. Real of Gen. Santa Cruz. Obv., Mountain; Rev., Dove with olive branch; "Peace, Union," etc.; also ½ real of Bolivar, 1830. Nick near top. Otherwise fine 2 pieces

980 1839. Cuzco. ½ Dollar. The employés of the mint to Marshal Gamarra Obv., View of an impending battle. Fine

981 1789. Proclamation real of New Guatemala. Cavalier over mountains ; also one 1808 for Santa Ana. Pierced as usual 2 pieces

982 1833. Honduras. Necessity 2 reals. Tegucigalpa mint. First issue as a State. Uncirculated

983 1867. Mexico. 2, 1 and ½ reals of *Hermosillo* mint. Broad coinage. Fine 4 pieces

984 1767-1864. Haiti, Danish Indies, Mexico (Maximilian), and an odd French piece. Sizes 9 to 14 9 pieces

985 Mauritius. 25 sous. Treasury token. Good

986 Old Groat of Henry IV., King of Castile. Bust like on English groat. Rev., Castle in a rose; " Enricus quartus rex." Good and desirable

987 1066 A. D. Penny of William the Conqueror. Bust with sceptre. Rev., " Lifwine on Exct." WAXS in annulets. Fine and desirable

988 1272 A. D. Edward I. Pennies. Rev., " Vill. Sci. Edmundi "; also one " Civitas Cantor." Fine 2 pieces

989 1307 A. D. Edward II. Pennies. Canterbury. Good 2 pieces

990 1327 A. D. Edward III. Penny. " Edwardus." Rev., " Civitas Dunielmie " (can find no record of this spelling of Durham), a cross-crozier; coined by Bishop Hatfield, 1345-81. Good and desirable

991 1758. George II. Penny. Fine and sharp

992 1770. George III. ½ Crown for Brunswick, and Bilston 6d token. Good 2 pieces

993 1808. George III. Irish thirty pence or ½ crown. Good

994 1799. Pius VI. Necessity Crown of 60 Baiocchi, struck at Fermo, during his retreat from Napoleon. The scarcity of silver is shown by the predominance of copper in these coins. Very fair. Size 24

995 1848. Frankfort. Thaler or 2 gulden of Duke John of Austria. Struck in commemoration of the final Parliament at that city. Proof

996 1690. France. Louis XIV. ½ Crown. Sun above, date below bust. Good

997 1831. France. Henry V. 1 franc. Bust to left as King. Pin scratch in field. Otherwise fine

998 1833. France. Henry V. Small copper. Head to left. Very fine

999 1534. Poland. Sigismund I. Groat. Bust to right. Title of Lord of Prussia. Fine

1000 1614. Poland. Sigismund III. Groat. Large crown. Also Groschen of 1731. Fine   2 pieces

1001 1831. Poland. 10 groszy. Struck under Prince Czartoriski. Uncirculated

1002 1835. Republic of Cracow. 5 and 10 groszy. Fair and proof   2 pieces

1003 1223. Turkey. 5 and 10 piastres. Long inscriptions on each side, within circles of flowers. Very fine and broad. 18 and 22   2 pieces

1004 1255. Turkey and Egypt. ½, 1 and 2 piastres. Good to fine.   6 pieces

1005 1274. Tunis. Piastres formed into a very pretty breastpin. 6 coins around a star. Fine and curious

1006 Japan. Oblong Itzebue and ¼; Hong Kong 10c., and 1841, 2 annas. All uncirculated but one   4 pieces

WASHINGTON AND LINCOLN MEDALS.

Fine unless otherwise stated.

1007 1834. Washington. Large bust to left, surrounded by names of 7 Presidents and Lafayette. Rev., Large eagle on shield and scroll. Pewter. Fine original.   Size 32

1008 Washington. Head to right. By *Davis* (Birmingham). Rev., Arms of N. Y. State. White metal. Pierced. Rarely seen. Size 16

1009 Washington. Naked bust to right. Rev., 12 stars; copper, size 9; also ¾ faced bust. Rev., Stoner & Shroyer's card. White metal. 12   2 pieces

1010 Washington in wreath. By *Wright & Bale*. Rev., their card; also one, same head facing that of Lafayette. Copper and german silver. Sizes 12 and 17   2 pieces

1011 Washington with hand on shield, facing Grant. Eagle and motto above. Rev., 8 line inscription in wreath. White metal. Pierced. 27

1012 Washington to left. "The pattern of patriotism." Rev., 8 lines in palm wreath. Bronze. Only 12 struck. Size 18

1013 Washington to left in wreath. "The father of our country." Rev., Same as last. Bronze. Only 12 struck. 18

1014 Washington to left. "In God we trust," above. Rev., Same as last. Bronze. Only 15 struck. 18

1014a Martha Washington in wreath. Rev., Same as last. Bronze. Only 12 struck. 18

> N. B.—The dies of the above four medals were separated several years ago, NEVER to be used together again.

1015 Washington to right. Rev., "Time increases his fame." Silver from U. S. Mint. 18

1016 Washington to right. Rev., Mount Vernon; also one with rev. blank. White metal. 22   2 pieces

1017 Washington. Different portraits. Pierced. White metal. 18 and 22   3 pieces

1018 Washington bust on pedestal between officer and soldier of 7th Regt. White metal. 28

1019 Lincoln. By Key. Rev., A. L. on broken column. White metal. 32

1020 Lincoln. "Honest Old Abe." Another, bust of Johnson facing. Another bust to left. "The Martyr President." White metal. All unpierced. Unusual in this condition. Sizes 20, 21, 26   3 pieces

1021 Lincoln. PRESIDENT. The best I've seen of this. Another by Smith. "War of 1861" below. Brass. 17 and 19   2 pieces

1022 Lincoln. Busts to right. Rev., Flying eagle; Rev., Indian head; Rev., ½ bust Washington; Rev., "Lincoln and Union." Heads to right; Rev., F. Lehr's card; Rev., Bust of Washington. Heads to left; Rev., "America"; Rev., "FREEDOM"; Rev., FREEDOM; O. K. in chain. Copper, brass, white metal and german silver; all size 12. The most desirable lot of Lincoln's I ever sold together   10 pieces

BUNKER HILL MONUMENT MEDALS.

1023 1840. Monument surrounded by rays and clouds, "Sept. 8." Rev., Death scene of Gen. Warren. White metal. Original. Pierced. Good. Size 27

5^- 1024 1840. Eagle above monument, flags, arms, &c. "Sept. 10," "Harrison Jubilee." Rev., Head of H. to left. White metal, silvered. Original. Pierced. Fine. Size 27

$/8$ 1025 Monument, "A nation's gratitude." Rev., Bust of Harrison to right; "The hero of Tippecanoe." Peacock bronze. Very fine. Size 24

2 1026 Same obv. as last. Rev., Bust of Clay in oak wreath, by *Thomas*; "The farmer of Ashland." Peacock bronze. Very fine. 24

$/5^-$ 1027 1843. Monument; trees and houses; "Completed June 17th." Rev., Flying eagle with banner, etc. Peacock bronze. Fine. Pierced. 16

$/5^-$ 1028 1775. Monument, view of Boston. Rev., Shield inscribed "June 17th, 1775;" WARREN above all in a wreath. White metal. Pierced. Fine. 17

20 1029 "1875. June 17th," in curved line below monument. Rev., British soldier thrusting bayonet at fallen Warren. Fine. Bronzed. Pierced. 17

$/2$ 1030 1875. Radiated monument. Rev., Monogram of 7th Regt., N. Y. N. G. White metal. Fine. 20

20 1031 Monument; gilt facsimile, worn as a pin at celebration. Fine. 28

35^- 1032 1875. Charlestown Antique Ass. Obv., A tolerable portrait of the President with ballast shifted. Zinc, plated; always pierced. Size 40

COLONIALS, Etc.

$/5^-0$ 1033 1794 Franklin Press ½d. "Sic Oritur Doctrina Surgetque Libertas." Fine

25^- 1034 1794. "Liberty and Commerce," (rev. of Talbot Allum and Lee cent.) Rev., Small bust of John Howard. Very good. Fine for the piece, and desirable

$2/$ 1035 1787. N. J. cent. Obv., "Nouia 1776 Esarea Britan 1787." Rev., Shield across Geo. III.'s bust, "Luribus Unum III. Rex." Sharply struck and a remarkable combination

1036 1787. N. J. cents. Sprig under bust; 8 obliterated by broken die; also a very fine but pierced specimen, before die broke   2 pieces

1037 *Auctopi* Connec. Rev., incused, but not opposite letters on obv. Good. Curious

1038 1740 and '58. Louisiana sixpence and shilling; m. m. A. and X. A very fine pair 2 pieces

1039 1787. Franklin cent. Numerous rays around sun. Rev., a raised 8-pointed star between States United. Good and unlike any I've seen

1040 1787. Nova Eborac. Female seated to left. Fair

1041 Vermont, Mass., N. J., Connec. and Constellatio cents. Ordinary lot 8 pieces

1042 1855. Struck copy of U. S. cent. Rev., "Not one cent, but just as good." Semi-circle on each side, formed by die collar

1043 1836. *February* 22. First steam coinage. These were never restruck like the March 23 pieces. Gilt. Nick on rev. Very good

1044 1858. Eagle cent, struck in copper; drift marks visible owing to weak impression. I never saw a duplicate

1045 Nickel cent pattern. "One Cent" in wreath. Rev., blank. Proof

1046 1799. Cent., altered; fine misstruck cents; and bronze cent, no date nor legend on obv. 4 pieces

1047 1878. 1, 3 and 5 cents. Proof set

1048 1846. Dime. Very good and sharp impression. But little circulated

1049 1851. Silver Three cents. Uncirculated

1050 1853. Silver Three cents. Uncirculated

1051 1855, '59, '61 and '63 Three cents. Former good; others uncirculated 4 pieces

1052 1866. Silver Three cents. Proof not brilliant but sharp

1053 1869. Silver Three cents. Uncirculated. A beauty

1054 1870. Silver Three cents. Proof

1055 1871. Silver Three cents. Proof surface

1056 1872. Silver Three cents. Proof

OLD STORE CARDS.—(*No Restrikes.*)

1057 Baker, Canal St., N. Y.; Erwin, Cinti., O., and Eckstein, Jr., soda. All have U. S. eagle on obv Fine 3 pieces

1058 Bowen & McNamee, and Scoville Manf. Co. Obv., eagle. good 2 pieces

ᕑ 1059 Beals, Boston; and Ruggles, N. Y., by *Bale*. Copper; one pierced. Very good   2 pieces

⎿ 1060 Richardson, W. H., and W. & Co., 104 and 106 Market St., Phila. Fine   2 pieces

⟶ 1061 Milton, Boston "Faneuil" and "Faneuil;" Mechanics' School, by *Wright* and Richards, 1834. Fair to fine 4 pcs

♂ 1062 Mitchell and Tyson, stage tickets, and Reed St. Ferry. 2 oval; ger. sil., brass and cop. Very good   3 pieces

♂ 1063 Elliott, Vinson & Co., Memphis. Rev., "Our rights," etc.; and Jaccard & Co., St. Louis. White metal and brass. Fine   2 pieces

ᕑ 1064 Stoner & Shroyer. Rev., Franklin in cap. Rev., Grant; and Cheviot 25c. ticket. Cop. and w. m. Fine. 3 pieces

♂ 1065 Person's Calendar; Coup's Circus; Robbins, Royce & Hard. Various metals. Fine   6 pieces

♂♂ 1066 1837–1857. Satirical on Hard Times, "Never keep a paper dollar in your pocket till to-morrow." 2 sous; fat and lean sows. White metal. Proof. Size 22

♂♂ 1067 1838. So-called Hard Times token. Obv., a hive and bees (or pigeons); date below. Rev., a vine wreath. Fine. Copper. Size 18

4 1068 1862. Postal-metallic currency, 1c. and 5c. Rev., Advs. Mendum, etc.   5 pieces

/ 1069 Centennial cards and Mear's Erie seals   4 pieces

♂ 1070 Centen. cards of Moses H. Moses & Co., Vesey St., N. Y. Rev., Indep. Hall. Rev., Lib. bell. These cards were rejected and all but a few destroyed. White metal. Proofs. Size 24   2 pieces

CENTENNIAL MEDALS, &c.

GO 1071 1875. April 19th. Lexington minute man; farm scene in background. A fine medal, bronze. 24

♂♂ 1072 Centennial Legion. Names of 13 States. Obv., Shield, flags. Copper. Proof. 20

♂♂ 1073 Lafayette. Bust to right. Rev., N. Y. statue unveiled 1876. Fine. 20

♂♂ 1074 1876. Hayes. Bust, ¾ face; "THE" in large letters. Rev., Wheeler, "Centennial." White metal. Pierced. Good. Very few known. 20

- 1075 1876. Hayes; similar to last, but different dies. Copper. Also, Harlem Plains and German visitors Centennials. White metal. 20 to 28   3 pieces

2-1076 Centen. Fountain ; comma after " Fountain ;" not many struck; also, the common variety, with different spacing. Cop. gilt. Proofs. 24   2 pieces

6 1077 Pottsville, Pa., Centen. Tea Party, and Cape May Ball, 1876. White metal. Fine   2 pieces

3 1078 The most horrible Centennials. Obv., Spreadeagle. Obv., Bell. Brass and lead. Fine   2 pieces

2-1079 "Centenial." Ind. Hall, with buildings on each side. Maltese cross-shaped " July 5 ;" and cards. Copper and white metal. Pierced   5 pieces

- 1080 Duplicates with heads of Washington. Pierced. White metal   32 pieces

-- 1081 Masonic. Fine helmeted head to left. Rev., " Hommage de FFF ∴ MAC ∴ D'EUROPE 5876," etc. Beautiful bronze proof. 24

-6 1082 Masonic. Bust of Washington to right. Rev., "Initd in Fredericksburgh Lodge, V., Nov. 4, 1752." Silver. Fine. Only *four* thus altered. Size 17

.'1083 Masonic. Bust of Washington, designed from his death-mask. Rev., K. T. motto. White metal. Proof. 52

2 1084 Masonic. Central Am. Lodge. One, Washington, by Soley. Rev., Emblems, and N. Y. Temple dedication. Copper, bronze and white metal. All proofs   4 pieces

- 1085 Chosen Friends Lodge. Gilmore's Maltese cross ; Camden Philotechnic and Turner medal. All fine. Copper and white medal. 16 to 32   4 pieces

2 1086 Kossuth. One with 12 line inscription on rev. ; and Fenian John Mitchel. White metal and brass. Very good. 18   3 pieces

1087 1871. Jim Fisk. Rev., Locomotive ; 9th Regt., Co. C., Armory ; Wright's medal of Alexander the Actor, 1847 ; and Prince Albert. Fine. Copper. 15 to 20   4 pieces

2' 1088 1682. Penn's treaty with Indians, and 1842 the Constitution disabling the Guerriere. Silver and gold plated. Fine. 20   2 pieces

1089 Maj.-Gen. Anthony Wayne. Rev., "Stony Point," etc. White medal. Proof. 22

5 1090 Racehorses. Flora Temple and a stallion. Rev., Cupid on dolphin. Unusual reverse. White medal and brass. Fine. 18   2 pieces

5 1091 Great Eastern and Atlantic Cable. Beautiful peacock bronze. 20   3 pieces

// 1092 S. P. C. A and Firemen's Medals. Brass and white metal. Fine. 20 to 32   3 pieces

25 1093 National Rifle Association Prize Medal for Creedmoor. Bust of Mars. Copper. Fine. Very few struck. Size 25

55 1094 1846. U. S. Coast Survey. The meanest medal issued at the mint. Bronze. Fine. 21

30 1095 1781. Battle of Cowpens. Ordered by U. S. for Col. Howard. Fine. Bronze. Original. Struck at Paris. 29

30 1096 1784. Dupre's fine bust of Franklin. Rev., A *male* angel, with broken emblems of royalty at his feet. A fine bronze medal. Original. 29

25 1097 1833. Barre's Franklin and Montyon. Struck by the French Society. Bronze. Fine. 26

10 1098 Bale's N. Y. College Medal. Rev., " Virt. et dil. praem." Fine. Desirable. Bronze. 17

10 1099 "Confederation." Fire altar amid stars, beneath radiant eye. Rev., "Continental Currency." Fine. Bronze. 24

12 1100 Virginia State Award Medal. Large. Fine. White metal. Size 47

2 1101 Nashville, New York and Cincinnati Exposition Medals. Brass and white metal. Fine   4 pieces

5 1102 1847. Sons Temperance; Amer. Juvenile Temp. Soc.; Union Reform Asso.; and one, a woman feeding a tramp, with glass of water (never saw this before). White metal. Fine. 20 to 24   4 pieces

2 05 1103 OBSCENE. Obv., Society Cupid. Rev., Modern Venus. Engraved on nickel cent planchet

2 40 1104 OBSCENE. Obv., Stock Exchange Bull. Rev., Stock Exchange Bear. Engraved on nickel cent planchet

The above two pieces are about as bad as it has ever been my misfortune to run across.

ANCIENT GREEK AND ROMAN COINS.

1105 Hyrium, in Campania; Didrachm; head of pallas; rev., the Minotaur walking to right, *ΓΡΙΝ* above: these letters are negative, and are read the same as type; very good and remarkable

1106 Epirotes, in Epirus; Didrachm; head of Jupiter; rev., Eagle on thunderbolt. *ΑΠΕΙΡΩΤΑΝ*. Fine and well struck; desirable

1107 Sicyon, in Achaia; thick Hemidrachm; the Chimera walking to left; *ΣΙ* below; rev., flying dove; fine

1108 Histeia, in Euboea; Hemidrachm; a Bacchante to right; rev., a female seated in a sail-boat, a bell and *ΙΣΤ* below: typical of the Trojan's favorite harbor; fine

1109 Argos, in Argolis; Hemidrachm; half a wolf to right; rev., Caps of the Dioscurii below *Α*, *ΤΡΓΙΙΙC* ; good

1110 Macedonia, 323 B. C. Drachm of Philip III.; head to right; rev., Jupiter with eagle; *ΦΙΛΙΙΙΙΟΓ*; good

1111 Judea, 54 A. D.; bronze lepton of Nero and Britannicus; rev., date palm; fair

1112 Judea, 58 A. D.; bronze lepton of Claudius Felix; straight palm; rev., inscription in wreath; very fair

1113 Egypt, 67 A. D. Potin Tetradrachm of Nero Claudius; rev., bust of Juno; obv., weak rev., fine; desirable

1114 Egypt, 66 A. D. Another Tetradrachm but head to right; rev., head of Africa in elephant's headdress; very good

1115 Rome, 14 A. D. Denarius of Augustus; head to r.; "Caesar" on left; rev., a *Cow* standing. "Augustus" above; a very unusual reverse; good

1116 14 A. D. Augustus, 2d bronze, one with portrait; "Augustus Tribunic. Potest" in wreath; well patinated
2 pieces

1117 12 B. C. Marcus Agrippa, Tiberius and Titus; 2d br., fair to good
3 pieces

1118 79 A. D. Vespasian; Denarius; rev., the Emperor seated holds an olive branch; very good

1119 117 A. D. Trajan. Denarius; rev., female with branch; a camel at her feet. From the fact that the Jewish silver of Agrippa are always struck over denarii of this type, it is supposed that these were coined for Judea; very good

1120 138 A. D. Hadrian, Denarius; very large head; rev.,
Annona seated before a modius of poppy-heads; very
good

1121 138 A. D. Hadrian, 1st and 2d br. also 2d br. of Domi-
tian; good   3 pieces

1122 161 A. D. Antoninus Pius, Denarius; fine portrait; rev.,
female with corn taken from a modius on a prow; fine

1123 161 A. D. Antoninus Pius; 1st and 2d br. good   2 pcs

1124 138 A. D. Antoninus pius, Denarius, head to right; rev.,
youthful portrait of Marcus Aurelius; struck on his adop-
tion; very good and desirable

1125 180 A. D. Marcus Aurelius, Denarius, with title, " Armen-
iacus," in full; very good; also, 2d br. fair   2 pieces

1126 192 A. D. Commodus, 1st br.; rev., Victory seated, (the
Vict. Britannica) and one with Com. on a raised platform
distributing gifts to the people. "Lib. Aug. IIII."; fair,
but historical reverses   2 pieces

1127 211 A. D. Septimus Severus, Denarius; rev., Domna
standing; fine

1128 238 A. D. Caius Maximinus I., Denarius; fine portrait;
rev., his son between Army Standards; very fine

1129 244 A. D. Gordianus III.; Denarius; very fine portrait;
Emperor seated holds a flower; very fine

1130 249 A. D. Philip the Arab; Denarius; fine sharp portrait; rev., female with caduceus; very fine

1131 250 A. D. Etruscilla; Denarius; fine portrait on a crescent;
rev., Pudor veiled; this Empress is only known by her
coins; fine

1132 284 A. D. Numerianus; 3rd br.; rev., "Virtus Augg."
Num. and his father, Carus, standing; green patination;
very fair and desirable

1133 1st, 2d and 3d br. of Alexander, Maximin, Maxentius,
Victorinus, Crispus, etc.; also a Consular denarius; fair
to good   14 pieces

MEDALS, Etc., FEDERAL AND CONFEDERATE, RELATING TO THE REBELLION.

1134 22d Regt. N. Y. Veteran medal. 1865. Obv., fasces (for Brooklyn) on which hangs shield with arms of U. S. and N. Y. State. Mottoes above and below. Four flags at sides. Rev., "Military Merit." Name in circle of pellets. A very beautiful medal struck in Paris. With clasp attached. Silver. Very fine. 21

1135 21st Regt. N. J. Veteran medal. State arms in circle of stars. Rev., "Presented to Capt. J. W. Low." With clasp. Silver. Very fine. 22

1136 Loyal National League. Maltese cross decoration. Beautiful bust of Liberty in centre. Loop at top. Plated. Size 24

1137 30th N. Y. Brigade. "Death to Traitors." Rev., names of ten battles. W. M. Fine. 25

1138 Heads of Washington. Rev., "No Compromise with Traitors." Nickel and cop. Good 2 pieces

1139 1861. "Concession Before Secession." Obv., "We the People of," etc., on scroll. Nickel. Fine

1140 1860. "Not One Cent for Slavery." Rev., eagle. Brass. Very good. 15

1141 1862-3. Maj.-Gens. Pope, Grant and Berry. Copper. Fine. 15 and 18 3 pieces

1142 Maj.-Gen. Sherman. Busts to left and right. Cop. and W. M. Fine. 20 2 pieces

1143 Union envelopes ; various designs ; some used. No duplicates 25 pieces

1144 Gallery of Traitors. Rev., names of Floyd, Bell, Davis, Stephens, Breckenridge, Thompson, Toombs, Cobb, Maury and Wise. W. M. Fine. 21

1145 Envelopes with portraits of Davis, Stephens, Toombs, Floyd, Maury and John C. Breckenridge. Fine portraits 6 pieces

1146 Bust of Breckinridge to left. Rev., "No Submission to the North." Palmetto, 15 stars, cannon, etc. Copper. Fine. 14

1146a Bust of Breckinridge. Rev., "The Wealth of the South." Sugar-cane, cotton, etc. Brass. Fine. 14

/2   1147   Head of Breckenridge to left. Rev., "Our country and our rights." Peacock bronze. Fine. 15

25-   1148   Elliot. Vinson's card, Memphis. Rev., "No Submission to the North." Palmetto, etc. Brass. Fine. 14

22   1149   "No Submission to the North." Small cannon and 7 balls. Die cracked. Rev., cotton, etc. Brass, plated. Pierced. Very desirable. 14

40   1150   "No Submission to the North" Larger cannon and 6 balls. No period after "North." Rev., similar to last. Brass. Fine. 14.

35-   1151   1863. Lieut.-Gen. T. J. Jackson. Fine portrait. Rev., names of 22 battles. Very fine. W. M. 32

FOREIGN COPPERS.

/7   1152   1697. England. Wm. III. halfpenny. Very good. Fine for piece

40   1153   1713. Anne farthing. Rev., Britannia seated. Somewhat circulated and I believe, a counterfeit

/2½   1154   1750. Geo. II.; and 1831, Wm. IV. halfpence. Fine. Latter rarely found so good   2 pieces

5-   1155   1731. Russia. Dengui and 1811, 2 kopecks. Very good   2 pieces

45-   1156   1657. Griffon on pedestal. Rev., sun above rose bush. Fine

55-   1157   1677. Half-length figure of Charlemagne. Rev., fleur-de-lis on shield. Fine

40   1158   1689. Ship under sail, "Boutevillain," etc. Rev., a bishop. Very good

25-   1159   1791. Azores. 10 reis of Maria I. Very good. Size 23

20   1160   1813. Essequebo. Half stiver, Geo. III. Very fine. Olive color

25-   1161   1816. Isle de Bourbon. 10 centimes ; and Cayenne, 1789, 2 sous. Good and fair   2 pieces

25-   1162   Louis XIII. Bust to left. Rev., a lion holds a rabbit before a cock. Fine

25-   1163   Louis XVI., 1792. 2 sous. Bell metal. Fine

20   1164   1855. Head of Satan. Rev., card of the famous actor Voisin. Bronze proof. Size 13

22   1165   1773. Moldavia-Wallachia. 2 paras. Also small coppers of Poland and Romania. Fair to fine   3 pieces

35·1166 1831. Greece. 10 lepta of Count Capodistrias. A phœnix beneath a cross. Fine

15 1167 1851. Greece. 1 and 10 lepta of Otho. Very fine. 2 pcs.

5 1168 1819. Ionian Isles. Farthing; and 2 lepta of Geo. I., Greece. Good and fine 2 pieces

20 1169 1870. Spanish Republic. 1 and 5 gramos. Fine. 2 pcs.

15 1170 1859. Tuscany. 1 and 5c. of Victor Emanuel. Fine 2 pieces

5 1171 1816. Canada. Sir Isaac Brock token. Fine and sharp

20 1172 1820. Portrait medal of Jean Varin, Intendant General of Canada. Bronze. Very fine. 26

35 1173 1779. Owhyhee (Hawaii). Bust of Capt. Cook, discoverer of Sandwich Islands. Fine. W. M. Size 24

12 1174 Lot of foreign coppers—Asia, Africa, Europe and America. No duplicates 125 pieces

14 1175 Another lot No duplicates 90 pieces

12 1176 Another lot. Not so good as last. No duplicates. 75 pcs.

A FEW CHOICE POLITICALS, Etc.

30 1177 "Gen. Andrew Jackson." Rev., "The Nation's Pride." Uncirculated. Peacock bronze. Seldom found so fine. Size 15

25 1178 Similar obv., different die. Rev., "The Nation's Good." Uncirculated. Peacock bronze. 15

15·1179 Another bust. Three-quarter face to right. Rev., "Hero of New Orleans." Initials in field, otherwise fine, pierced. 15

1180 Head Jackson to left. Rev., "U. S. Second Term, Mar. iv., 1833." And a funeral medal. Silver and W. M. Fine. 12 and 18 2 pieces

1181 Harrison. Bare head to right. "The Hero and States man." Rev., log cabin; smoke issuing to left. Beehive on right. Pierced. Original. Very fine

1182 Clay. Busts to left and right. Rev., monument; rev., "Tariff." W. M. Fine. 12 and 27 2 pieces

1183 Cass. Busts to right and left; former by Wright. Rev., Freedom of Seas; rev., Sub-Treasury. W. M. Fine. 21 and 26 2 pieces

1184 Taylor, by Wright. Fine portrait. Rev., "A Little More Grape." W. M. Proof. 20

1185 Grant, Lieut.-Gen. Bearded head to left. Rev., 5 lines between stars. Silver. Proof. 12

1186 Grant, Hayes, Tilden and Seymour. Cop., W. M. and celluloid. Fine. 12 to 16   6 pieces

1187 McClellan. "Candied-date," and Bridgen's tokens. 4 reverses. Copper. Uncirculated   6 pieces

1188 Pin badges of Garfield, Hancock, Lincoln, Greeley and Tilden   10 pieces

1189 1881. *Gold.* Garfield bust to right, dividing date. Octagonal ; like Cal. half dollar. Fine. Size 7

1190 *Gold.* Garfield. Rev., bust of Mrs. Garfield. Octagonal; like Cal. quarter dollar. Size 6

1191 Garfield Inaugural Ball ticket. Portraits of Garfield, Arthur and Washington. Exceedingly fine steel engraving, with additional admit ticket. 6 by 9¾ inches

1192 Garfield Inaug. Ball Programme. Lithog. in colors ; 10 pages. 4½ by 6 inches

1193 Garfield Memorial portrait ticket for Blaine's eulogy, Feb. 27, '82. A beautiful steel engraving by the National Bureau. 6 by 9¾ inches

1194 James A. Garfield. Statuette bust in porcelain. Nearly full faced. A striking likeness. 12 in. high; across shoulders, 8 in. Small stand at bottom 2½ in. high, 4¼ in. wide, on which is a scroll with fac-simile of Garfield's signature. Made in England. A beautiful piece of workmanship, tasty in design and very desirable

1195 Old pistol and sword point from Mexican war   2 pieces

1196 Steel die for U. S. 12c. envelopes ; present issue. Defaced

1197 Old bank notes and Confed. shinplasters. All different   31 pieces

1198 U. S. 3c. currency. Dark curtain behind Washington. Uncirculated. 3 notes unseparated

1199 A Canadian political coin (the "Vexator Canadensis") pamphlet. Ottawa, 1874. One illustration

1200 Jewitt's Handbook of English Coins; from the conquest to present. Concise descriptions. 11 colored plates. London, 1879. Cloth

www.ingramcontent.com/pod-product-compliance
Lightning Source LLC
Chambersburg PA
CBHW022037080426
42733CB00007B/870